EZRA POUND

COLUMBIA INTRODUCTIONS TO

TWENTIETH-CENTURY

AMERICAN POETRY

JOHN UNTERECKER, GENERAL EDITOR

EZRA POUND

AN INTRODUCTION

TO THE POETRY

SISTER BERNETTA QUINN, O.S.F.

COLUMBIA UNIVERSITY PRESS

NEW YORK

PUBLISHER'S NOTE

Just as this book was about to go to press, Ezra Pound died in
Venice at the age of eighty-seven. Although certain statements by
the author regarding Pound were thereby made inappropriate, it
was decided to present Sister Bernetta Quinn's introduction to Ezra
Pound's poetry as she designed it. Hopes for the future may have
been snuffed out at Pound's death, and the present tense have
slipped into the past, but Pound's writings and the spirit of this
book remain very much a part of the living.

Library of Congress Cataloging in Publication Data

Quinn, Mary Bernetta.
    Ezra Pound; an introduction to the poetry.

    (Columbia introductions to twentieth-century
    American poetry)
    Bibliography: p. [179]–184
    1. Pound, Ezra Loomis, 1885–1972 I.   Series.
PS3531.082Z788   811'.5'2   72-6830
ISBN 0-231-03282-X

Printed in the United States of America
10 9 8 7 6 5 4 3 2

TO OUR LADY OF SILENCE

COLUMBIA INTRODUCTIONS TO
TWENTIETH-CENTURY
AMERICAN POETRY

Foreword

Ezra Pound sometimes seems less a writer than an entire literary community, one that has accidentally assembled in the body that goes by his name. Editor, poet, anthologist, critic, propagandist, cultural historian, English teacher, he has also been called patriot, traitor, sage, madman, defender of the artist, corrupter of the young. The list could go on and on.

The temptation, in such a situation, is to discover an "essential Pound" in a few of his themes or, even more conveniently, to dismiss the man entirely and focus on a close reading of one work: the Mauberley poems, say. Nothing, however, could be more destructive of what Pound set out to accomplish. Like his friend Yeats, he worked very hard indeed to see that essays, letters, historical studies, poems, translations, even anthologies, were parts of a single mosaic that would become *the work*. Unlike Yeats, who had the good fortune to guide through the press one collected edition of all his works and to project, shortly before he died, another such edition, Pound has had the misfortune to see plans for one after another collected edition fall through. Though James Laughlin of New Directions has managed to keep much of Pound in print, the definitive collected works seems still to be light years away. Pound, the only man really competent to make the final selection, revision, and sequencing of such an edition, is almost certainly no longer capable of so monumental a task.

What we are left with, therefore, are the unassembled fragments of a design that Pound was never able to put into final shape.

And yet what fragments they are! Even the reader of the *Selected Poems* is bound to be struck by Pound's extraordinary facility, his capacity to sound casually "right" in forms that range from Anglo-Saxon verse structures to the most intricate Italian, Provençal, or French ones.

What makes this facility possible is something that is less learned than innate: Pound's ability to hear and to reproduce the most subtle nuances of speech. Pound talked a great deal about the importance of the poet's sense of verse melody—the delicate weave of sound and accent that plays above the stress pattern of a line and that imposes on that pattern an author's unique voice. It is this sure ear for verse melody, I think, that makes us swear by the "rightness" of a great deal of Pound's work—whether in his own poetry (most conspicuously perhaps in the Pisan Cantos), his editorial activity (most conspicuously perhaps in his cutting of Eliot's *The Waste Land*), or his translations (most conspicuously perhaps in the translations from Li Po).

Once we have accustomed ourselves to this voice, then we are ready to discover the ways in which individual elements of Pound's work interconnect: the melodies of the Chinese, the Provençal, the Italian translations weaving into and through the historical and contemporary "events" that accent

The Cantos, melodies that fuse in a mind like waves washing into and over each other, interpenetrations of light:

> What whiteness will you add to this whiteness,
> > what candor?

Pound asks. He is writing Canto 74, the Pisan Canto that catalogues the deaths of his friends Yeats, Ford, Joyce—three of the greatest writers of our time. He has not yet reached the passage that touches on their deaths, however, and he answers his question most obliquely:

> and there was a smell of mint under the tent flaps
> especially after the rain
> > and a white ox on the road toward Pisa
> > as if facing the tower,
> dark sheep in the drill field and on wet days were clouds
> in the mountain as if under the guard roosts.

His mind moves from those whitenesses to the whitenesses of wild birds, of Carrara stone, and of the "light of light":

> in the light of light is the *virtù*
> > "sunt lumina" said Erigena Scotus
> > as of Shun on Mt Taishan . . .

It is in passages like this that directly precede his meditation on the death of Yeats and Joyce that our ear picks up the melody of earlier work—the translation of Li Po's "Exile's Letter," for instance, that great account of a friendship broken by the accident of time and place:

> And if you ask how I regret that parting:
> It is like the flowers falling at Spring's end
> > Confused, whirled in a tangle.
> What is the use of talking, and there is no end of talking,

> There is no end of things in the heart.
> I call to the boy,
> Have him sit on his knees here
>   To seal this,
> And send it a thousand miles, thinking.

The melodies weave in and out, though half a lifetime separates their dates of composition, and though twelve hundred years separate Li Po from Yeats, Joyce, and Pound.

Sister Bernetta Quinn brings to her compassionate introduction to Ezra Pound not only a scholar's erudition but a most sensitive reader's insightful knowledge of the art of poetry. Her *The Metamorphic Tradition in Modern Poetry* is one of our most valuable contemporary literary studies. Her recent work has focused primarily on symbolic landscape in modern poetry. Sister Bernetta, a member of the faculty at the College of St. Teresa, Winona, Minnesota, is a visiting professor in English at Allen University, Columbia, South Carolina.

Preface

No man is ever merely what he is at any given stage of his life-span. Ezra Pound is more than the octogenarian with snowy leonine mane and sharp blue eyes waiting out his time in European exile; he is more than the inmate of Saint Elizabeth's Hospital lounging on the lawn amidst a handful of disciples or staring out of his window in the bare Chestnut Room; more than the *maestro* of Rapallo, arranging concerts, begging magazine acceptances for his unsung contemporaries; more than the archenemy of convention in Paris; more than the highly intelligent senior at Hamilton College. In the mysterious manner of art, *The Cantos* contains elliptically and in its own dimension all that he is or has been, while each of his other books, like a talking mirror, gives back some part of the exuberance and Mozartian gaiety characteristic of him before the advance of old age. *Drafts & Fragments of Cantos CX–CXVII* captures in abstract that "interior landscape" he now inhabits, a country beyond the threshold of silence.

The present book endeavors to give a straightforward account of Ezra Loomis Pound, the man and the poet, including, I hope, insights and facts not appearing elsewhere. The work of other scholars has been invaluable in providing a context for details. I am indebted to the Foundation of the Humanities and the Foundation on the Arts for grants which enabled me to undertake research and travel between February, 1967, and August, 1968. The kindness of the Princess Mary de Rachewiltz, both during my stay at Brunnenburg and later, has been a supportive influence for which I am sincerely grateful. I wish also to acknowledge all that I owe to Donald Gallup and Norman Holmes Pearson of Yale University in terms of counsel, friendship, and interest. Finally, I would like to thank Sister Emmanuel Collins, O.S.F., Mary Barnard, Mrs. Carl Gatter, George Nix, Bruce Nichols, to mention only a few, whose encouragement and assistance have furthered the completion of this introduction to Ezra Pound.

The approach in the following pages is based upon Saint Augustine's "Love so that you may understand." It is designed to lead new readers to Pound's verse and to illuminate passages for those already acquainted with *il miglior fabbro*. This poet is a man who can rightfully take to himself that line from his own "Propertius": "Yet the companions of the Muses will keep their collective nose in my books." His is truly a name of the future, one "not to be worn out with the years."

Sister Bernetta Quinn, O.S.F.

May, 1972
Allen University
Columbia, South Carolina

Acknowledgments

Acknowledgment is gratefully made to New Directions Publishing Corporation for permission to reprint from the following works by Ezra Pound: *The Letters of Ezra Pound, 1907–1941*, edited by D. D. Paige, copyright 1950 by Ezra Pound, reprinted by permission of New Directions Publishing Corporation; *The Cantos of Ezra Pound*, copyright 1934, 1937, 1940, 1948, © 1956, 1959, 1962, 1963, 1965, 1966, 1968, 1970 by Ezra Pound, reprinted by permission of New Directions Publishing Corporation; *Personae*, copyright 1926 by Ezra Pound, reprinted by permission of New Directions Publishing Corporation; *The Translations of Ezra Pound*, copyright 1954 by Ezra Pound, reprinted by permission of New Directions Publishing Corporation; *The Spirit of Romance*, all rights reserved; *ABC of Reading*, copyright 1934 by Ezra Pound; *The Literary Essays*, copyright 1918, 1920, 1935 by Ezra Pound, reprinted by permission of New Directions Publishing Corporation; excerpts from previously unpublished letters by Ezra Pound, copyright © 1972 by Ezra Pound, published by permission of New Directions Publishing Corporation, agents for the Committee for Ezra Pound.

Acknowledgment is also made to Faber and Faber Ltd., for permission to quote from *The Cantos, Personae, The Translations of Ezra Pound, ABC of Reading,* and *The Literary Essays,* all by Ezra Pound; to Doubleday & Company, Inc., for permission to quote from Homer, *The Odyssey,* translated by Robert Fitzgerald, copyright © 1961 by Robert Fitzgerald, reprinted by permission of Doubleday & Company, Inc.; and to Harcourt Brace Jovanovich, Inc., for permission to quote from *Selected Letters of E. E. Cummings,* edited by F. W. Dupee and George Stade.

For permission to quote from unpublished letters, thanks are due to the Princess Mary de Rachewiltz; Viola Baxter Jordan; Mary Barnard; and Alfred Rice, Esq., on behalf of the estate of Ernest Hemingway.

Finally, for permission to quote from letters in their respective collections, acknowledgment is made to the Rare Book Department, Free Library of Philadelphia, and the Beinecke Rare Book and Manuscript Library, Yale University Library.

Contents

CHAPTER 1

Ezra Pound the Man

A shock of white hair, piercing sea-blue eyes, the strong delicate hands of a sculptor—Pound in his San Ambrogio apartments (the familiar maize scarf emblazoned MAKE IT NEW
around his shoulders) or walking along a quai of Venice's San
Gregorio has about him a nobility which seems to reach back
to Confucius in his cedar grove near the lower river of the
temple grounds; and long before that, to Sophocles by the
black waters of the Aegean. It is hard to imagine how anyone
so courteous and gentle could have attracted the enmity
which has frequently characterized press comments on him.
Dante in exile tasted the same bitter bread, yet today the
quiet corner given over to him near Ravenna's Franciscan
church stands as symbol of the transcendence over the vaga-
ries of Fortuna which Pound appears to have attained even in
this life.

Born in Hailey, Idaho, on October 30, 1885, Ezra Loomis
Pound was named after a fifth-century B.C. high priest of the
Jews, and after his paternal grandmother, Susan Angevine
Loomis. The family name had originally been Lummyus: an
ancestor, Thomas Lummyus, died in Thaxted, England, in

1551. From the union of Susan Loomis and Thaddeus Coleman Pound, the poet's father, Homer Loomis Pound, was born in 1857.

"T.C.P.," as *The Cantos* calls Pound's grandfather, served as a member of the United States Congress and also as lieutenant governor of Wisconsin. A resident of Chippewa Falls in that state, he saw the importance of monetary systems to human happiness as second only to peace (he and his wife were Quakers). As a supporter of the Greenback party platform, Thaddeus favored government control of money. Canto 103 describes him as trying in the 1880s "to keep some of the/ non-interest-bearing etc./ in circulation/ as currency." Rightly is this spirited leader of the people placed by his grandson among the thrones, since, as Paul A. Olson says: "Pound's just men are all law-makers in their way." [1] After the death of Thaddeus, Susan Angevine made her home on Estaugh Street, Philadelphia, where Ezra must frequently have visited and listened to stories of pioneer days in the Midwest. His youthful admiration for "T.C.P." helped direct his own passion for justice, which was to grow in the years when the difficulty of earning a living kept constantly before him the problem of faulty distribution of wealth.

In 1884 Homer Pound, who had married Isabel Weston, brought his young bride from her home in New York City to the frontier settlement of Hailey, Idaho, now known chiefly as Ezra Pound's birthplace. It is linked to his integrity in an epitaph which Rex Lampman, a fellow patient at Saint Elizabeth's Hospital, wrote as foreword to the 1958 *Pavannes and Divagations:* "Here he lies, the Idaho kid,/ The only time he ever did." The move, initially intended only as a trip, became a job opportunity. William Sievert writes: "Homer Pound had come to Hailey to look after his father's [Thaddeus's] properties, silver mines, and went on to become the Recorder of the Government Land Office." [2]

Before their baby was three years old, Homer and Isabel left Hailey, via Wisconsin, for Pennsylvania, where the future poet's father had obtained a position as assayer in the Philadelphia Mint, work not entirely dissimilar to what he had done in Idaho. For two years the family lived at 208 South 43d Street. Their home was a brick row house, since converted to apartments. Their next location was a temporary dwelling in the suburb of Jenkintown, after which they settled down in a simple frame house at 166 Fernbrooke Avenue in the adjoining Wyncote. So rich in memories is this white house on the hill that Pound has twice come back to renew them since his departure from Saint Elizabeth's. Though much is different, a few things remain, such as the black armchair carved with animal figures which stands today just inside the front door; it was one of the objects unsold after Mrs. Homer Pound's impulsive auction at the time she and her husband left Pennsylvania permanently to take up residence in Italy with Ezra.

From the age of six or seven, Pound attended the Chelton Hills school conducted by the Heacock sisters Elizabeth and Annie, an experience which he recalled sixty years later in his correspondence with Mrs. Carl Gatter and her son, currently occupants of 166 Fernbrooke Avenue. [3] In these letters he emphasizes his fondness for his teacher Florence Ridpath, whose career he kept in touch with into the days of her retirement. Next he enrolled in the Cheltenham Military Acad-

emy in Elkins Park (or Ogontz), Pennsylvania, where Freder-
ick James Doolittle soon became for him another admired
teacher. At the news of Doolittle's death, Pound wrote Carl
Gatter: "I am sorry 'Cassius' is no longer. He was a fine bit of
old oak." [4]

Not enough critical attention has centered on the fact that
Pound grew up on the outskirts (sometimes in the midst) of
that most American of cities, Philadelphia, the nation's capital until 1800. The site of the Liberty Bell and of the room
where the Declaration of Independence was signed, the place
is alive with patriotic associations. Almost every building
must have spoken of his country's political origins to his vi-
sual imagination.

Back in Wyncote, Ray, the name that community still
knows him by, had an ordinary enough boyhood. Its highlight was an 1894 trip to Venice and other romantic spots
with a great-aunt, souvenirs of which are preserved in *The
Cantos*. To expand the family income, the comfortable house
on Fernbrooke Avenue was shared with a few paying guests,
among them a maiden lady, Miss Clara Warren, and her
mother.[5] Mr. Pound regularly traveled home from the mint
on the Reading Railroad, while each night Mrs. Pound
watched for the sight of him returning so that she could walk
out to meet him. Their mutual affection was far from the
"sundered parentage" of Hart Crane's youth; on the contrary,
it offered a welcome stability to the talented only son. The
approximately two thousand letters out of which editor D. D.
Paige selected a sampling include a warm picture of the candid, witty relationship existing among the three Pounds

which can be projected back to earlier days when presence made letters unnecessary.[6]

After Ezra entered the University of Pennsylvania at fifteen, his student-friends enjoyed either gathering around the piano in his home to sing while Isabel played or engaging in what was a favorite recreation in that house, conversation. Without ever becoming intimate with her, the town admired the somehow quaintly out-of-place elegance of the mother, who centered her life on an intense devotion to her husband and their brilliant only child. Everyone thoroughly liked the good-natured father, just as all who came to see Ezra during the Rapallo years held Homer in the highest esteem for his geniality, wide interests, and humor.

Homer's duties at the mint on Spring Garden Street held a constant attraction for his son, as recorded in Canto lines like "In the gloom the gold gathers the light about it." Opened in 1901, the building is a short distance from the University of Pennsylvania, not too far for a pleasant walk. Its importance to the father all but made nomads out of him and Isabel: several times, when their son was absent at school or in Europe, they moved in from Wyncote to be near it. The various city directories of Philadelphia list as addresses for them 502 South Front, 2103 Spring Garden, 1834 Mount Vernon, 1640 Green.

While it would have been pleasant for the family to have remained together throughout Ezra's undergraduate days, after two dissatisfied years at Penn he transferred to Hamilton College in upper New York State. Climbing the miles-long hill from the town of Clinton toward the Hamilton campus was like entering a rural paradise in comparison to approaching his former university surrounded by city streets. His first year there, Pound lived in Hungerford, a very old building of wood and stucco which had been erected in the 1820s. So dilapidated was this structure that it was torn down the year after Pound left. As a junior he had to endure primitive living conditions: no indoor plumbing and lighting by gas jet, although there was heat for the students willing to lug coal up to their rooms at twenty-five cents a bucket. The next year he moved to Carnegie, a brand new dormitory which, according to the college catalogue, was among the nation's most luxurious, with private baths and electricity. Pound's suite was on the fourth floor front in this building, which looks very much today as it did during his residence.

The school itself, rising high above Clinton and nearby Utica, had been founded in 1793 as an academy for Indians. What life was like there between 1903 and 1905 can be visualized in part from the lively letters of Pound's fellow students Ned and Clarence Day.[7] The grounds were truly beautiful. Oren Root, a relative of Elihu Root, whom Theodore Roosevelt had chosen as Secretary of State after the 1904 political landslide, had landscaped acres of descending greenery behind what is now the Root Art Center. In Root Glen anyone seated on a bench beneath a mountain ash or sprawled on the grass watching the changing clouds might feel as shut off from the rest of the world as Marvell in his garden. On the quadrangle above, the chapel, decidedly ornate in Pound's day though recently simplified, offered another quiet retreat to the upperclassman from Wyncote, not ostensibly pious but always grateful for a place where he could think the long thoughts of youth, to paraphrase a line from one of his ancestors, Henry Wadsworth Longfellow. Not by any means a joiner, he did participate in Hamilton's chess team, winning honor for the college by his skillful playing. Like the other boys he very likely enjoyed rousing up the old Irish lady, Madame Kelly, who sold penny candy and ices in her little shack and who could never resist the hungry youthful patrons flocking to the store even afterhours.

More attracted to books than to sports, Pound was nevertheless usually ready for a fencing match or some tennis, both of which he had practiced in Wyncote. In tennis he occasionally took on his favorite professor, Bill Shepard. Shepard it was who introduced him to the troubadour poetry of the Middle Ages, for which George Putnam's descriptive guide was to become his Baedeker.[8] His major medieval enthusiasm, however, was Dante, about whom he wrote his mother from Hamilton in February of 1905: "He was incidentally a poet a lover and a scholar and several other trifles served to round out his character although it is not recorded that he was President of a U.S. steel trust or the inventor of pin wheels."[9] His boyhood correspondence, such as this letter, has none of the facetious oddities in spelling of later periods or the abbreviated, fragmentary style which reached its ultimate in the telegraphic communication of the Washington days.

Among the courses Pound took during his stay at Hamilton were psychology, German, Latin, English literature, French, Italian, Old English, Spanish, Provençal, the Bible, economics, logic, English and American history, physics, sociology, rhetoric, debate, trigonometry, analytics, parliamentary

law, and what at the time was called elocution. But the
heavy program of studies which he carried never prevented
him from seeking amusement. Viola Baxter Jordan, an old
friend of his, writes:

I met Ezra at a dance in Utica where I lived. He was 19 or 20.
Being an only child, when he was in Hamilton College he came to
Utica one day looking for diversion I suppose. He came to see me
and I went with him to the college doings.[10]

The tumultuous days of the Roosevelt administration can
hardly have left unmoved an undergraduate as politically
alert as Pound. T.R., at the height of his vigor in his forties
when he entered the White House, proved that he could do
battle not only on the military field but against the wealthy
monopolists who were threatening the economic justice of the
American system. In him Pound had an early example of a
"throne," a heroic man spending the best of his great talents to
guard the principles of public integrity. *The Cantos* eventually was to give ironic praise to historians who left spaces
for what they did not know. In accordance with this, the present volume can only suggest an attraction that fighter
"Teddy," President from 1901 to 1909, might have exerted on
Pound.

Hamilton's regard for its greatest alumnus has been demonstrated by its awarding him an honorary degree in 1939, by
the honor it publicly paid him at the 1969 Commencement,
and by its readiness to invest large sums in library holdings
bearing on his career. Pound has returned its esteem by frequent gifts of books, magazines, and letters, as well as by
traveling to its campus on the two occasions when he received its homage.

After receiving his Ph.B, Pound resumed work at the University of Pennsylvania, this time for a Master's degree. Not all of his memories of that institution were negative. It was here that he met H.D. (Hilda Doolittle), the dryadlike daughter of a professor of astronomy, and also the medical student to whose widow he was to telegraph in 1963: "He bore with me for sixty years," disclaiming any hope of finding another friend such as William Carlos Williams. Philadelphia compensated for the loss of Hamilton's woodland beauty by its stirring monuments of our American origins. Often Pound must have walked across the city to see that symbol of freedom the Liberty Bell, encircled with the tenth verse of Leviticus, 25: "Proclaim liberty throughout all the land unto all the inhabitants thereof." Whatever of United States history exists in *The Cantos* can be called Ezra Pound's way of implementing the message of this landmark of independence.

In those days, Dr. F. O. Childs held forth in Old English in the Penn graduate school, and Dr. Felix Schelling in Shakespeare. The latter was to become a tie between the campus and E.P., though neither he nor Childs kindled the younger man's love of learning as Hamilton's William Shepard and Joseph ("Ibby") Ibbotson had done. Another professor at the time was the scholar in Spanish literature Dr. Hugo Rennert, enshrined in *The Cantos* together with the many other figures who then and later made up the quotidian texture of its author's experience: "And old Rennert wd. sigh heavily/ And look over the top of his lenses" (Canto 28). The doctoral program as a whole failed to stimulate Pound, though his insatiable curiosity continued to enrich his background in the medievalism which he was later to open up to countless poets.

Then came the opportunity, through a George Leib Harrison Fellowship in Romanics, to pursue research on Lope de Vega in Spain, followed by study in Italy and France. His parents shared in his picaresque adventures as these were humorously related in letters home and were as disappointed as he when the grant was not renewed for a second year.

Faced with the need for job-hunting, Pound settled on teaching as the occupation least likely to interfere with his literary tastes. The Yale collection of Paige letters shows him delighted with having "nailed" a position at Wabash College in Crawfordsville, Indiana, where he was to have the Department of Romance Languages to run as he pleased. In the beginning the situation was agreeable enough. Through the mails he carried on a courtship with Mary Moore of Trenton, New Jersey, whom he had come to know in 1907; this affair came to a sudden end when she became engaged to someone else.[11] But Wabash as the months went by proved to be far from ideal for a faculty member who might be styled "an apostle of diversity."

Dismissed in 1908 because of narrow administrative interpretation of an act of kindness he had extended to an itinerant entertainer, Pound shook the dust of Indiana from his heels and went off to London on the salary due him by force of his contract. From the capital of England he wrote Homer L. in January of 1909: "Being family to a wild poet ain't no bed of roses but you stand the strain just fine" (Yale American Literature Collection, henceforth abbreviated as YALC). The prose rhythm of this sentence reveals an ear praised by Babette Deutsch: "No living poet exceeds his gift for keeping astride two horses at once, one foot firm on the back of direct colloquial language, the other foot as firmly planted on the back of the melodic phrase." [12]

Pound's removal to Europe introduced him to several congenial persons, the most impressive of whom was Mrs. Olivia Shakespear, "undoubtedly the most charming woman in London," as he described her to his mother in January of 1909 (YALC). He had met her, with her daughter Dorothy, through a series of lectures which he was giving at the Royal Polytechnic Institute in order to support himself. Through the Shakespears he came to know William Butler Yeats. As a matter of fact, it was largely the magnet of Yeats's genius which had drawn him across the Atlantic to the British Isles in the first place. One evidence of his admiration is his sending Yeats, in 1908, an inscribed copy of *A Lume Spento*. The rapidity with which their friendship developed bears witness to the American's outstanding qualities of mind and character. It was a friendship destined never to lapse.

Other relationships multiplied: Hugh Selwyn Image, Laurence Binyon, Victor Plarr. But the Shakespears—the socially talented mother and Dorothy, classic in profile and dedicated to painting—remained "quite the nicest people in London," as he wrote his father.[13] Gradually he was detaching himself from the homeland: he sent back to America for some of his favorite books, such as the *Poem of the Cid*, Aristotle's *Poetics*, the Moore edition of Dante. With extraordinary thoughtfulness he reported his social life to the parents left behind in Pennsylvania in a way which brought vicarious excitement into their days: an evening with an English nobleman who promised him his personal copies of *The Divine Comedy;* tea with the publisher Elkin Mathews, who offered an entrée to the most noted men of letters in the city; a luncheon where he acted as escort to Ellen Terry; attendance at a meeting of the Poets' Club in George Bernard Shaw's company; a growing intimacy with Plarr, whom he was to commemorate in that eclectic synthesis of this stage of his progress through Europe, "Hugh Selwyn Mauberley." Most satisfying of all was the time he spent with "the leading poet to use the English language in this century," though this appellation had not as yet been conferred on him. "Yeats is in town again & I shall see him at the Shakespear's on Wednesday," he wrote to his mother,[14] and then:

Yeats left this morning for Dublin. He is the only living man whose work has anything more than a most temporary interest—possible exceptions on the continent—. I shall survive as a curiosity. The art of letters will come to an end before A.D. 2000 and there will be a sort of artistic dark ages till about A.D. 2799.[15]

Underneath the comment, of course, is a good-humored jibe at the Platonic year, a jovial tribute to the visionary propensities of his elder contemporary.

Occasionally friends and relatives arrived to be "toured." In March of 1910 he showed William Carlos Williams the artistic side of London, taking him to see Yeats and also London's famous Turner paintings. His life as free-lance writer and lecturer permitted holidays in France and Italy. In the latter country he felt a genuine devotion to Verona, with its Church of San Zeno, monument of a faith which seemed more admirable to Pound than the fundamentalism he had left behind when he sailed from his native shore. He regarded as an image of Paradise the *paese* of nearby Lake Garda, on the banks of which "the haunt of Catullus," Sirmione, is situated.

The year 1911 found him in Paris, sharing an apartment with the musician Walter Rummel,[16] one of the first of those who were to set Pound's lyrics for vocal or instrumental rendition. During this year the friendliness with Yeats grew closer: "Yeats I like very much, I've seen him a good deal, about daily," he wrote home, adding that the Irish poet "is as I have often said before, a very great man." [17] The sweetheart (to the point where they were informally engaged) of his University of Pennsylvania days, the poet H.D., had appeared in London; she wrote back enthusiastically to Isabel Pound about Ezra's tremendous hospitality.[18] The rapturous mood of "Night Litany" informs these years—excursions to Mantua, Ferrara, Ravenna, Rimini, Bologna, Pistoia, Lucca, Siena, Rome. Pound's preparation through reading and his sensibility made it possible for him, wherever he journeyed, to fathom centuries-old picturesqueness of architecture and the richness of troubadour song.

By March of 1912, he was writing to his mother from 10 Church Walk in Kensington, urging her to keep up with his intellectual life of lectures and galleries: "Before embarking on these affairs, I advise you to fortify you mind with the simplicities of Aristotle & Aquinas" (YALC). What another parent would have found patronizing Isabel accepted in good part. This period in his life is well covered in Patricia Hutchins's *Ezra Pound's Kensington*, especially useful for its account of Ford Madox Ford. Ford, originally Ford Madox Hueffer, learned in chess as well as in Provençal and other literatures, proved a wonderful companion for Pound, one whose conversation and writing he never ceased extolling.

Not yet thirty, Pound had published enough verse, both

original and translated, to win him acclaim and to rejoice his family: *A Lume Spento, Personae, Ripostes, Exultations, Canzoni.* Of special interest is *A Lume Spento,* with its dedication to the artist-friend of his Penn days, William Brooke Smith, of whom so little is known though a warm attachment existed between them not severed by the young painter's death. A rose from the Hamilton College bud, *The Sonnets of Guido Cavalcanti* began a long series of probings into this Tuscan lyrist so admired by Dante. The proficiency in languages which had facilitated Pound's premature entrance into a university curriculum expanded with each new poetic discovery, ancient, medieval, or modern. Like that other expatriate writer Henry James, Pound now made his living largely by the pen, a very sparse living, true, but brightened by the hospitality of a circle of artists. These afforded him a society nonexistent in the United States, where before he left for Europe the only editor to encourage his ambitions was Witter Bynner of *McClure's Magazine.*[19]

American writers abroad invariably sought out Pound's lodgings. Robert Frost, whose first book appeared in England for lack of interest at home, never had a more energetic or influential supporter than Ezra Pound. The factor which "made all the difference" to his poetic stature might well have been the confidence Pound instilled into him. Indefatigably Pound went into action, securing Frost favorable notice by critics, neglecting his own projects to do so. On June 3, 1913, he wrote his father: "I'll try to get you a copy of Frost. I'm using mine at present to boom him and get his name stuck about" (YALC). It is true that later he came to believe Frost had not developed according to the early Kensington expectations: his

1932 anthology, *Profile,* makes clear this disappointment by rating the New Englander as inferior to Crabbe, though "infinitely better than fake." [20] In an interview with Hans Beck for the *Paris Review,* Robert Frost demonstrated himself to be guilty not only of a ludicrous oversimplification of the efforts of friends to extricate Pound from Saint Elizabeth's but also of a strange disregard of personal benefits received. "He wrote me a couple of letters when I got him out of jail last year," Frost flippantly said. Then he went on to describe in a vein of jocularity the climax of years of cooperative endeavor by Pound's supporters:

Well, I went down after we'd failed and after Archie MacLeish thought we'd failed, I just went down alone, walked in the Attorney General's office and said, "I come down here to see what your mood is about Ezra Pound." And two of them spoke up at once. "Our mood's your mood; let's get him out." Just like that, that's all. And I said, "This week?" They said, "This week, if you say so. You go get a lawyer and we'll raise no objection." So since they were Republicans, I went over and made friends with Thurman Arnold, that good leftish person, for my lawyer. I sat up that night and wrote an appeal to the court, and, in the morning, just before I left town, I wrote another one, a shorter one. And that's all there was to it. Ezra thanked me in a very short note that read, "Thanks for what you're doing. A little conversation would be in order." [21]

But a "little conversation" with the great poet who had already suffered behind locked doors for thirteen years was too much trouble for Frost, who never saw him again. The reason he gave to interviewer Beck for not acceding to Pound's request was, "I didn't want to get high-hat with him." [22] Friends and family accepted Frost's gesture gratefully. The day before Frost died, Pound's daughter, the Princess Mary de Rachewiltz, went to see him in the hospital to thank him for the tardy afternoon and evening he had given to the un-flagging campaign which she, MacLeish, Eliot, and others had been carrying on for more than a decade. Human behavior is hard to understand: perhaps subconsciously Frost was still smarting a little from the memory of his role as Mr. Nobody in the presence of the scintillating impresario of Church Walk. However that may be, the poet *did* take action, precipitating the long-overdue release.

For three winters Pound retired with Yeats to a stone cottage in Sussex, a setting uncongenial to his city-loving disposition. In the country, however, the two scholars had leisure to enjoy the English classics. "We are reading Landor and the autobiography of Herbert of Cherbury, both with enjoyment," Pound told his mother in a December letter of 1914 (YALC). His candid reactions to the Celtic Twilight helped transform it into the "hard cold light" that Yeats was soon to attain. Quite unmoved by the unique privilege of sitting at the older man's feet, Pound treated him as an equal, and the days of reading aloud and discussion passed agreeably for both.

In 1914 Pound announced to Wyncote that he was planning to marry Dorothy Shakespear. The message was as casual and unromantic as possible, its tone matching the matter-of-fact, almost staccato style characteristic of communication among the Pounds:

I dare say I am going to be married. The family has ordered the invitations and stuff for curtains, etc. In which case I shall *not* come to America and if you want to inspect us you will have to come over here.[23]

From this comment, it would seem obvious that he had been contemplating a trip to Pennsylvania; his terse summons of his parents might well have been his way of expressing a certain homesickness and a need for their presence.

At this time Pound was still living in an out-of-the-way corner of Kensington in an upstairs flat of the building at 10 Church Walk, since demolished and rebuilt. In this neighborhood today the only reminder of him is an occasional display of his work in the window of a bookstore now on the corner nearest to where he once resided. By March of 1914 he had moved to 5 Holland Place Chambers, from which center his incredible energy kept him in the forefront of the Vorticist movement, which he served through manifestoes, art criticism, constant promotion of the painters involved. This was the period of his translations of Noh plays, which preceded Yeats's more famous triumphs in that genre. It was also the era of discovering European contributors for Harriet Monroe's magazine in Chicago. Besides being foreign editor for *Poetry,* he acted in this capacity for *The Egoist* and *The Little Review.*

Arrangements for the marriage continued throughout that spring. To his mother he wrote: "The wedding is on the 20th of April. Then we go to the country." [24] The ceremony at Saint Mary Abbots, the lovely old building from the presence of which Church Walk took its name, was a simple affair. Mrs. Pound did come over later that year, not so much to "inspect" as to satisfy motherly affection and assuage her loneliness for Ezra, a natural emotion after her husband's retirement and before their permanent reunion with their only son. For economy's sake the place chosen for the honeymoon was the stone cottage of William Butler Yeats, where in the Sussex springtime the bride, D., as Ezra usually called her in letters, could happily cultivate her hobby of oil painting.

October of 1914 marked the poet's first meeting with T. S. Eliot. What that meant for the latter was dramatically revealed to the world by the 1968 discovery of the original manuscript of *The Waste Land* among the John Quinn papers: a miracle in transformation effected by the critical genius of Pound. The steady buoying up of Eliot's morale by his fellow American, both in person and on paper, is a story which can never be fully told. Other writers were similarly helped. Even before World War I, E.P. had begun his long-term tireless befriending of James Joyce by requesting poems from him for magazine publishing and for the anthology *Des Imagistes*. It was through Pound's urging that Joyce was awarded a grant from the Royal Literary Fund; moreover, out of kindness he strategically placed favorable reviews of the Irish writer in *The Egoist, The Future, The Dial,* and other periodicals to which he had editorial access.

Many Canto passages not now considered autobiographical will ultimately be recognized as such; some sections already are. Joyce, Eliot, Ford, Williams, all the companions of his youth have their parts to play in that tapestry of voices which is the whole epic. The third Canto presents him as a young man in love, sitting on the Dogana's steps in Venice watching the gondolas which are too expensive for his lean purse and appreciating the lights of the Morosini palace illumined for a feast day. Canto 20 re-creates the walking tour through southern France and elsewhere in Europe with Putnam's *Books and Their Makers during the Middle Ages* as mentor:

And that year I went up to Freiburg,
And Rennert had said: Nobody, no, nobody
Knows anything about Provençal, or if there is anybody,
It's old Lévy.

In Canto 80 the lifelong admirer of François Villon composes his own "Où sont les neiges . . ." with a lament for Nancy Cunard, A. R. Orage, Ford Madox Ford, René Crevel, Arthur Symons, W. B. Yeats, James Whistler, Gaudier-Brzeska, Carl Dolmetsch, Mabel Beardsley, John Quinn, Maurice Hewlett, each name a glimpse into a vanished world. Reflecting on its glories, Pound draws this moral for his daughter, Mary:

> Quand vous serex bien vieille
>   remember that I have remembered,
> mia pargoletta,
>   and pass on the tradition
> there can be honesty of mind
>   without overwhelming talent
> I have perhaps seen a waning of that tradition

Canto 16 concentrates on World War I, its toll of dead or wounded eulogized by a catalogue of real or changed names: Aldington, Gaudier-Brzeska, Hulme, Léger, Hemingway ("and Cyril Hammerton went to it, too much in a hurry,/ And they buried him for four days"). The poem also preserves small happenings, one example of which is a conversation with Frank S. ("Baldy") Bacon, profiteer in Cuban copper pennies and in insurance, who had come to Wyncote during Ezra's boyhood. About this colorful character he wrote his father: "Frank Bacon also turned up last week. Was damn glad to see him, after twelve years. Had just used part of his biography in my Cantos." [25] Canto 84 mentions Pound's trip home in an attempt to avoid international catastrophe by pleading with the lawmakers: "Thus the solons, in Washington,/ on the executive, and on the country, a.d. 1939." Elsewhere in the long poem, the poignance of the Pisa days and his filial care for little Mary come through in

> The black panther lies under his rose-tree.
> J'ai eu pitié des autres.
>   Pas assez! Pas assez!
> For me nothing. But that the child
>   walk in peace in her basilica,
> The light there almost solid. (Canto 93)

A book-length analysis might well place into a narrative context a series of organized flashbacks from Pound's own life in the form of rearranged quotations from the Cantos. Such a story would render the man even more accurately than do his letters or the memories of those whose lives crossed his. No sensitive reader of, say, Canto 116 can fail to see the possibilities of such a project.

In the year 1915, his first as a husband, E.P. wrote his father of how "Eliot has suddenly married a very charming young woman"; Wyndham Lewis has enlisted; Henry James, after two strokes, will never walk again; he himself is reading *Sordello*, "the best long poem in English since Chaucer," and struggling with the first five Cantos (YALC). In a spirit of raillery he kept his mother informed about the not-yet domesticated Yeats, in whose wedding to Georgie Hyde-Lees he was eventually to participate: "Yeats is buying the ruin of an Irish castle so I suppose he will in time disappear from the world." [26] (Because of the 1916 date of this letter, he could not have meant Ballylee in Galway; rather, he must have had in mind the Castle of the Heroes which Yeats as a bachelor had aspirations of acquiring as a center for Gaelic culture.)

Except for Pound's weekly columns of criticism (art and music), he and his wife would have been indigent. These appeared under the pseudonyms of William Atheling and B. H. Dias, perhaps because his qualifications for the post were somewhat more informal than the London subscribers would have approved. Yet poor as was his income, Dorothy and Ezra traveled widely on the continent, for instance in the pilgrimage through Troubadour Land which they made in 1919. Unlike Mauberley, Pound did not let what "the age demanded" frustrate him. On the contrary, he made the best of his European holidays, learning from every place where he and his wife stopped how to make the old new and constantly experimenting with verse techniques.

By the 1920s, the Pounds were in France as residents. Ezra tried through Homer to get a Ph.D. degree from the University of Pennsylvania on the basis of the scholarly work he had done since leaving the graduate school. Had this application met with success, economic pressures would have been·lessened, but then so might have been his creative output, were he to have gone into the academic world. Unlike Hamilton College, the University of Pennsylvania, which has collected the books and papers of his classmate William Carlos Williams, has never shown any marked regard for Pound's association with it, apart from its faculty's interest.

A letter which E. E. Cummings wrote from Paris to his parents in July of 1921 gives an authentic picture of Ezra Pound at this period:

If it would amuse you:Mr. Ezra Pound is a man of my own height, reddish goatee and ear whiskers, heavier built, moves nicely,temperament very similar to J. Sibley Watson Jr. (as remarked by Thayer)—same timidity and subtlety,not nearly so inhibited. Altogether,for me,a gymnastic personality. Or in other words somebody,and intricate.[27]

These impressions, tightly constructed as a lyric, convey a stamp of approval which was never to be withdrawn.

Though technically Pound belonged to the "lost generation" abroad, he seems to have remained apart from it. He never frequented the salon of the lady who gave it its name, Gertrude Stein. Rather, he kept his own evenings, in the Montparnasse section, and was far from being "lost" as he and his cameo-featured young wife moved among such artistic figures as Brancusi, Cocteau, Picabia, Picasso, Berenson, Antheil, Léger. His friendliest connection among the expatriates was with Ernest Hemingway: "I play tennis with Hem two or three times a week," he informed Homer on September 12 of 1924 (YALC). The game helped relax him from his intense concentration on the Cantos, now approaching the end of their second decade (tennis, like chess, links together all the episodes in Pound's life from boyhood till old age). Before too long, the capital of France with its frenetic gaiety began to seem hardly the likeliest place wherein to compose his masterwork.

In 1924 the couple settled down for good in the small Italian town of Rapallo, described thus by Stephen Shorter: "Here you are confined in a strip of flat shore land by olive-covered mountains which rise immediately behind you and crowd you into the sea, the Ligurian Sea, or, more precisely, the Gulf of Tigullio." [28] Rapallo is at the northern end of the Riviera. During the twenty years ahead, one guest after another arrived to enliven with good talk the apartment which the Pounds chose on the Via Marsala not far from the water.

In this seashore resort, the poet was able further to indulge the passion for music which he had shown in England and France by sponsoring select concerts. One of the finest performers in Rapallo's series was the violinist Olga Rudge, "reviver of Vivaldi," and like himself an American who preferred to live abroad though without giving up her citizenship.

On July 9, 1925, his daughter, Mary, was born. This child, who was to grow up to be the loveliest poem Pound ever wrote, was early confided to a remarkable peasant woman at Gai in the Italian Tyrol. Her life there was more like that depicted in Dylan Thomas's "Fern Hill' than a girlhood in the intellectualized milieu of Rapallo. After she attained womanhood, she became a sensitive and meticulous translator and critic of her father's writing.

A happier, healthier Eliot spent his Christmas vacation of 1925 in the Via Marsala, arriving again in the spring of 1926 with his wife Vivian to occupy the Pounds' flat while they were away. In the fall of that year, on November 18, Omar Pound was born.

Intermittently during the next five years Pound made progress with the Cantos. By 1930 *A Draft of XXX Cantos* appeared through the Hours Press in Paris. Reading the book today, one can readily understand what prompted Hemingway to write Pound from Key West: "If there was any justice in this woild you'd have gotten the Nobel prize. You'll get it yet. I was damned sore." [29] Hemingway himself was to win it in 1954. During the interval Pound had published *The Pisan Cantos,* which alone should have justified Hemingway's confidence by gaining him the award.

About securing such honors for himself Pound was quite indifferent, through of course he would have appreciated the monetary assistance. He has been called arrogant; the truth is that, despite his emphatic, even explosive prose style, he possesses a humility as endless as that praised by Eliot. Such a spirit informs this 1935 letter to a Chinese correspondent: "We are ALL very ignorant men. Thirty-five years of study serve but to make us mildly aware of the extent of our own ignorance of DETAIL" (YALC). The same self-depreciation occurs in a 1937 communication to the Japanese scholar Kitasono: "But my ignorance is appalling and my memory beneath contempt" (YALC). To Williams he writes: "I am doubly thankful for a friend who'll say what he thinks—after long enough consideration to know what he really thinks—and I hope I'm going to be blessed with your criticism for as long as may be." [30]

Even Williams, who remained almost all his days in Rutherford, did not escape having his patriotism questioned. But no American writer has ever had his loyalty to his country so attacked as Pound. Yet to the editor of *Poetry*, at that time Morton D. Zabel, Pound remarked:

H. J. at the end; and Eliot in mature prudence decided the citizenship was not worth having. I have never come to that, and I don't expect to; but whether this is attributable to qualities of HEAD, I shd. be loth' [*sic*] to say.[31]

As Pascal has well written, "The heart has reasons of which the head knows nothing."

Dorothy's mother, Mrs. Olivia Shakespear, was bringing up Omar in England. Isabel and Homer Pound had crossed the

Atlantic to establish themselves near their son in Rapallo.
The intimacy which united E.P. with Ireland's greatest poet
is demonstrated by Noel Stock's citation from the December
13, 1933, *Chicago Tribune:* "It is said that Mr. and Mrs. William Yeats will not return to Rapallo, as Yeats's work keeps
him in Dublin. The Homer Pounds are occupying his beautiful home, which is filled with original Blakes, Burne-Jones
and Gordon Craigs." [32] This news release was probably sent
by Pound himself as evidence of the esteem and companion-
ship of celebrities, denied him in the United States but ac-
corded him in his self-imposed "exile." The elderly couple
were cheerful additions to the family circle: his father could
still tap-dance at seventy-eight. At the same time they were a
financial burden increasing with time. In 1941 Pound wrote to
C. Pellizzi:

I think I said that I have my aged parents, old man 83 yesterday;
and not been out of his flat more than five times in two years.
Well, his cash WILL NOT arrive from the U. S. In fact he has only
had a couple of months of his pension. I think only one month
since last June. And his reserves have run out. (YALC)

One slender source of income was his radio broadcasts, on
random topics, made for less than a dollar each. These began
on December 7, 1941, and concluded on July 25, 1943, one
hundred and twenty-six in all. The monitoring which went
into the typescripts prepared from them was truly wretched:
one example is the mishearing of *low* for *Loeb* in the January
29, 1942, broadcast.[33] Scheduled late in the evening, the talks
ranged over subjects as varied as the American stage, Cummings, money, war. It was, of course, his views on the last-

mentioned which caused his arrest in 1945. Consistently
Pound attacked the Roosevelt administration, somewhat in
the manner that more recent critics have assailed the policies
of Johnson and Nixon. Another reason for condemnation of
his broadcasts was his strong language in regard to Jews,
though to Pound Jews were not so much representatives of a
race or a religion as economic agents. In speaking of them he
followed his idol Brooks Adams, of whom Daniel Aaron
writes: "The gold-bug or Jew or banker (he used the words
interchangeably) embodied the spirit of the modern, the genii
of money." [34] The first talk was prefaced with the guarantee
that Pound would not be asked to say anything against his
conscience as a citizen of the United States; others at intervals began with the same statement.

Light on this sad chapter of Pound's history emanates from
his correspondence with Lady Olivia Agresti of Rome. He
told her on January 21, 1954: "No as far as I remember I
never mentioned germany on Rome radio/can't of course remember every word of 600 and more discorsi" (YALC). She
wrote him in August of 1956: "Your fault is that you are too
faithful to the old American traditions in an age which has
become largely one of gangsters and political acrobats"
(YALC). Much of the trouble, as critics on Pound have
pointed out, lay in the almost complete black-out of commu-
nications from his native land, as well as from Germany.

The tragic events of 1945 will be treated in a later chapter.
It is enough to note here that because of these broadcasts,
made partly to support his family and partly to express economic policies that he believed underlay worldwide military

conflict, he was arrested at Genoa on May 5, 1945, held for months incommunicado at the Disciplinary Training Center of Pisa, and at last returned to his nation's capital. There, he was indicted for treason. Pronounced by four psychiatrists unfit to stand trial, he was confined to Washington's government hospital for the mentally ill, where he was to remain until April, 1958.

In the late 1940s his daughter, Mary, who had grown up in the beautiful countryside north of Venice, had married a young aristocrat, the Baron Boris de Rachewiltz. For a moderate sum they purchased a castle between Merano and Brunnenburg, in the Italian Alps, a structure dating from the Middle Ages. By hard work, combined with aesthetic taste, they turned it into a dwelling of great distinction, publicized today by most of the color postal cards of the vicinity. Here in 1947 Pound's first grandchild, Walter (Siegfried), was born, and a few years later the second, Patrizia. Becoming a "grand-pop," as he put it, was one of the major joys of Pound's Saint Elizabeth years, a gray chapter characterized by his own saying: "Birds do not sing in cages."

Mary never ceased to labor toward the goal of his dismissal. To the occupants of the Fernbrooke house in Wyncote she wrote: "I have made a home for him here & we have been waiting for 12 years now, how anxiously you can well imagine! According to the papers we seem to have reason for new hope. Thank you again for your kindness—it is such a blessing to come across good people."[35] More and more persons, from Dominican friars in England to poets like Archibald MacLeish in America, were working toward the same end as the Princess de Rachewiltz. The mayor of Florence, Giorgio La Pira, had requested help from Ambassador Clare Boothe Luce as early as October of 1955:

The poet Eliot considers him his master and all the critics of the world recognize in him the highest voice of American poetry.

Ezra Pound will be seventy on October 30, and I, in the name of the City of Dante, of that city which is still grieving for the decree of exile passed upon its greatest poet, in the name of the Florentine and Italian poets, which is in the very name of poetry, ask you to intercede with the authorities of his country, so that the poet-prisoner may be given his liberty on his seventieth birthday.[36]

Perhaps the most effective measure toward Pound's release came when Representative Usher L. Burdick from the State of North Dakota initiated an inquiry into the justification for Pound's detention at Saint Elizabeth's. At length, in the spring of 1958, after the incident starring Frost which has been referred to above, Pound was released and charges against him dropped.

For two months, in order to escape reporters, he lived in the apartment of Craig La Drière, then professor in the English department of the Catholic University of America and now at Harvard. La Drière had faithfully come to see him during his hospitalization, as had another Catholic University faculty member, Giovanni Giovannini. Just before leaving this country, Pound went back to Wyncote for an overnight visit and also to Rutherford to see the friend of his youth, Williams. Among the few who accompanied him to the *Cristofero Colombo* in New York's harbor was Norman Holmes Pearson of Yale, whose vacation trip to Santa Sophia is immortalized in *The Cantos*. With Mr. and Mrs. Pound sailed

Marcella Spann, a young woman whose studies had led her to Washington and who later returned to obtain a doctorate at the University of Texas in Austin in preparation for a career of teaching.

The return from exile was at last a reality. Though Italy meant another kind of exile, this time it was voluntary, and welcome.

The reception at Brunnenburg was overwhelmingly joyous. Yet despite the peacefulness of the castle and its surroundings, as well as the affection lavished upon him by the de Rachewiltzes, the Alte Adige region of Italy proved to be too dull for one who had always been a lover of the activity of cities. The poet left the medieval stronghold of Brunnenburg, dividing his time according to the seasons between Venice and Rapallo. With the passing of years he became increasingly silent. What he once wrote to A. Camerino about another American writer offers a partial explanation: he remarked in December of 1937 that E. E. Cummings was "a bloke who keeps quiet until he has something to say" (YALC). Today Pound's taciturnity is as puzzling as it is famous. Yet his alertness is undiminished; though not sociable, he exhibits constant kindness. His mode of existence seems symbolized by the fate of his favorite city, Venice, which every year sinks deeper into the sea. A young woman named Toni Lisetto, proprietor of the Cici restaurant where he often eats, once said: "Men like Signore Pound should never grow old!" While the privacy of his thoughts ought to be respected, those who sincerely care about his work cannot help wishing to interpret them—even to interrupt his meditations. His remoteness from readers across the sea makes him seem an abstraction rather than a person. Attempts to penetrate the transcendence of his advance years are seldom successful, though his aloofness disappears with certain old friends, as was demonstrated by the attention he paid Marianne Moore upon the occasion of the reception in his honor in June of 1969 sponsored by the Academy of American Poets in New York.

Pound has never lacked friendship, though it has been more abundant in good fortune than in bad. No friend remained steadier than Cummings: their relationship may stand as a "figure in the carpet." In reviewing *Selected Letters of E. E. Cummings,* Joseph Epstein confirms this devotion:

His loyalty to Ezra Pound, especially after Pound's radio broadcasts for Mussolini, was unwavering. He supported the beleagured Pound in every way: in print, with money when he was ill (though Cummings had little enough himself), and with large doses of simple friendship.[37]

Thirty-eight years after their first meeting, a letter from Cummings described it thus to biographer Charles Norman: "During our whole promenade Ezra was more than wonderfully entertaining:he was magically gentle,as only a great man can be toward some shyest child."[38] Soon afterward Cummings confided to his mother: "As you may know,I have for some years been an admirer of Pound's poetry: personally, he sometimes gives me a FatherComplex."[39] To anyone who knows how Cummings felt about his father, this is a compliment.

Ten years after the initial meeting with Pound, Cummings and his wife Marion had the Pounds as dinner guests in Paris ("[Ezra, son of Pound, Homer]," his host in a letter to his mother jokingly labeled the famous guest).[40] When Cum-

mings returned to his usual address at 4 Patchin Place in
Greenwich Village, correspondence between the two friends
continued to flourish. Mostly the epistles were word-festivals.
In one, only the business purpose appears in straight English:
"For the rest,I am proud to be 'translated' as you select. . . .
It is a pleasure to hear from you, sir!" [41] A lengthy and clever
letter dated January 2, 1935, briefs Pound on Manhattan hotels for a visit to America which never came off; its postscript
shows their closeness ("la signor [in] a sends congratulations
to the seafarer. Let's know when").[42] Most of the thirty-two
letters to Pound included in the volume of Cummings's correspondence sparkle with wit. A sad note, however, is struck in
the downward progression of their salutations: these go from
"Dear Pound" to "Dear E.P." to "Dear Yank" to "Dear Ezra"
to "Nuncle," reminiscent of Lear's address by his beloved
fool.

When Pound landed in New York on April 30, 1939, his
one trip home before 1945, personal contact replaced writing
in their relationship. Two years later, in October of 1941, the
way in which Cummings begins his letter witnesses to the
fact that the feeling between them remained cordial as ever:

whole,round,and heartiest greetings from the princess & me to our
favorite Ikey-Kikey,Wandering Jew.Quo Vadis, Oppressed Minority
of one,Misunderstood Master, Mister Lonelyheart,and Man Without a Country [43]

Unfrightened by the 1945 hearing with its consequence of in-
carceration, Cummings on April 25, 1947, opens a letter with
"Hearty CONGRATULATIONS from Marion&myself on your
GRAND-fatherhood!!" [44]

Besides bolstering Pound's morale by sense and sheer non-sense during several painful years, Cummings supported him in the controversy over the Bollingen Prize by his wire: "HEARTY CONGRATULATIONS TO THE CAPITALIST SYSTEM IN PARTICULAR AND ANDREW MELLON IN GENERAL." [45] He also wrote James Laughlin, whose New Directions press had brought out *The Pisan Cantos:* "there's one poet you publish;and he's very young—the youngest (am certain, rereading Personae) alive/congratulations." [46]

Cummings's attitude toward man suffering was quite different from that expressed in Auden's "Musée des Beaux Arts." He did not "pass by" but rather involved himself by visiting Pound on the lawn of Saint Elizabeth's. In June of 1952 he wrote him from Patchin Place: "Dear EP—/ 'twas good to hearseehug you." [47] Having designated a bluejay as emblematic of Pound, he ends the letter: "saw a silent bluejay l'autre jour;he sends you his swoopingest." [48] He returns again in October to the bluejay, a symbol of himself to which Pound refers in *The Cantos:*

We live in a little house,far from seive lies ation: civilization & a big BLUEJAY seems to be our chief mascot—a stalwart rascal,whose Hue [*sic*] give me Joy unmitigated:& who fears no crow or gull extant. I've already remembered him to you. [49]

Among all of the bluejay's attributes, it was his courage that Cummings was singling out, that courage unafraid of icy blasts, together with the beauty of its plumage flashing through a drab cloud of sparrows. The comparison was a little joke between them, a pseudo-metamorphosis concretizing a sturdiness well deserving of admiration.

Right up to the end of his life, Cummings maintained com-

munications. A 1954 letter begins "Multitudinous Monolith-
—/bonjour!" and tells of its writer's growing acquaintance
with Eustace Mullins, author of a book on Pound, *This Difficult Individual*, which was the result of three years of
daily association in Washington—a "charming fellow-mortal:
whose epitaph re thyself makes(in my humble opinion)him
already deathless." [50] When Cummings and his wife were va-
cationing in Venice and Florence in 1956 the last letter to
Pound, as included in the 1969 selection, was dispatched; it
ends: "but,O my friend!Italia somehow is Herself:& always
miraculous." [51] This enthusiasm for the landscapes of Pound's
expatriation was another strong bond between them.

Few critics trace the novelties of E. E. Cummings to the
influence of Pound. Yet he himself disclaimed his own experi-
ments in favor of the more major ones of the older man. He
told Charles Norman:

& please let me make something onceforall clear:from my stand-
point,not EEC but EP is the authentic "Innovator"; the true trail-
blazer of an epoch; "this selfstyled world's greatest and most generous literary figure"—nor shall I ever forget the thrill I experienced
on first reading "The Return" [52]

In this world of dog-eat-dog, of professional jealousy, these
two men were models of mutual encouragement.

Nonjudgmental, tolerant, Cummings did not find it necessary to agree with each of Pound's ideas. In a letter written
from Silver Lake, New Hampshire, he objects to joining a
group who wished to "rehabilitate" Ezra Pound: "If the man
has sinned, nothing you can say or do will make him sin-
less—and if you're trying to render the poet socially respect-
able, that's an insult;because no poet worth his salt ever has

given or ever will give a hangnail for social respectability. . . .
But whoever or whatever he may be,Ezra Pound most em-
phatically isn't Unanyone or Unanything." [53]

After Pound's arrival in Italy, Cummings writes zestfully to
Mary de Rachewiltz in 1962, the year he died, urging her on
in the translation of his poems and promising photographs of
his paintings; he closes "with love to the red squirrel as well
as to EP." [54] As a postscript he sends her a quotation from
Thoreau which might easily apply to her father:

The poet is no tender slip of fairy stock, who requires peculiar in-
stitutions and edicts for his defence,but the toughest son of earth
and of Heaven,and by his greater strength and endurance his faint-
ing companions will recognize the God in him. It is the worshippers of beauty,after all,who have done the real pioneer work of the
world. [55]

Besides his gift for friendship, Pound constantly revealed
his fidelity as benefactor toward fellow writers. To give the
sample which Frost says is all that an artist needs, I intend to
cite Mary Barnard, an aspirant in verse and Greek translation
who met Pound first during his 1939 voyage to the United
States. Besides her visits to him at Saint Elizabeth's, she saw
him three times after his return to Italy. In the following passage she describes the unselfish patronage she found in him:

I can only underline what other people have already said about his
generosity to the beginning writer. He criticized—sparingly—and
made suggestions of work to be done; he sent my poems to editors,
sent people to see me, sent me to see other people (Williams,
Cummings, M. Moore, for instance), even sent a copy of one of his
own books—no, I don't mean one he wrote, but one he owned—a
volume of a French music encyclopedia, from Rapallo to Vancouver, because he thought I ought to see it, and it wasn't available
here. [56]

Pound answered Miss Barnard's letters as soon as he received them, once writing twice on the same day. His kindness to her was not spasmodic, but steady. In the letter quoted from above she continues to reveal how his concern for her changed the whole course of her life:

Occasionally he teased or scolded, but his interest never seemed to flag, and I was only one of so many! When we did meet in 1939, I was out of a job and rather desperate. That afternoon he took me to see Iris Barry, then at the Museum of Modern Art, and "told" her to give me a job. She didn't, but she told her brother-in-law, Charles Abbott, about me, and he hired me as curator of the Poetry Collection at Buffalo. It was Pound who introduced me to people who got me into Yaddo. It was Pound who introduced me to the man who took my Sappho manuscript to California and got it on the road to publication after it had been turned down again and again.

It was also Pound who introduced her to James Laughlin, the publisher who issued her work in *Five Young American Poets 1940*.

From his seclusion at Saint Elizabeth's, Ezra drew up a complete itinerary for Miss Barnard's initial European trip—towns to see, hotels to stay at, museums and monuments not to miss, restaurants and dishes to try, even a wine list:

What a trip it was! Three months—Genoa to Rome to Venice to Genoa, with stops at Perugia, Florence, Verona, Vicenza, Ravenna, Rimini, and so on, including of course Brunnenburg!

The excursion lasted from mid-April to July, with a sojourn at Rapallo. Such a firsthand account of his goodness to a complete stranger is cause for astonishment. Miss Barnard comments, "I wrote to him in the first place out of the clear blue, from Vancouver, not knowing *anybody* who could help at all." Time and geographical separation have been unable to lessen the regard which Mary Barnard and Ezra Pound still entertain one for the other.

A book frequently recommended by Pound is Peter Goullart's *The Forgotten Kingdom*. Today he himself is king of that realm. His ménage is far simpler than the least affluent of those who write books about him. Cummings spoke prophetically when he used the term *metanoia* of him: his dignity born of suffering, a nobility obvious in *The Pisan Cantos* and in his present deportment, cannot fail to move. He now knows the answer, as he looks upon Venice, to that question asked by his youth in "Night Litany":

> O God of the night
> > what great sorrow
> Cometh unto us,
> > that thou thus repayest us
> Before the time of its coming

After such knowledge, he chooses the same response as in the early poem:

> Even as are thy stars
> Silent unto us in their far-coursing
> Even so is my heart
> > become silent within me.

For the "enormous dream" of *The Cantos* ("God's plenty," like Chaucer), another reply than silence is required of the world. So be it.

CHAPTER 2

The Poet as Preceptor

If a reader regards Pound's *The Cantos* as too formidable an introduction to his poetry, he can begin with the highly readable prose. Here the writer very often assumes the role of preceptor, a word stemming from *praecipire*, "to know beforehand," and, as applied to Pound, meaning one who promulgates working rules respecting the techniques of an art. The rationale of all that he has written is contained in his critical essays, a factor which renders them decidedly useful to one who wants to know Pound. Moreover, his ideas are so influential that they have changed the character of four decades in American letters, have truly given poems (as the name of his New York publishing house suggests) new directions.

Some years ago, a young Irish poet, Malachy Quinn, picked up a volume of Pound's criticism in the British Museum, knowing nothing of the author. He went on to the early poems, the translations, and finally *The Cantos,* each step throwing its light into the subsequent area. His experience is an encouragement to all other serious students of modern literature, whether or not they be fellow craftsmen (like Quinn), who constitute the audience Pound had primarily in mind when he wrote his articles, later collected into book form, or his books planned as such from their inception.

Pound himself in his early years considered his criticism more a form of rhetoric than a lasting genre of appraisal. T. S. Eliot, who edited Pound's essays in 1954, felt otherwise: he states his purpose in reprinting the pieces in these words:

. . . to regard the material in historical perspective, to put a new generation of readers, into whose hands the earlier collections and scattered essays did not come when they were new, into a position to appreciate the central importance of Pound's critical writing in the development of poetry during the first half of the twentieth century.[1]

Despite the absence of any evaluation of drama, no critic of our time, Eliot believes, can less be spared. He stresses the need to bear in mind the contexts in which the selections were written, none being produced in a vacuum or as ultimate; rather each is a landmark in the growth of a great sensibility. William Carlos Williams is at times credited with being the father of contemporary American poets. Never enthusiastic about Williams, Eliot takes a different position, calling Pound more responsible for the twentieth-century revolution in poetry than any other individual.[2] Pound's prose is much more lively than that of any other poet-critic of his age, brimming over as it is with apothegm, image, wit.

One of the greatest services Pound has done is to revive neglected authors, a service accompanied by attacks on established reputations if their makers have overshadowed finer men. His statements (sometimes pontifications) have weight in that he is never merely a theorist. He is capable of doing as well as of saying. Eliot praises the way in which Pound closes the gap between ideal and artifact:

And of no other poet can it be more important to say that his criticism and his poetry, his precept and his practice, compose a single *oeuvre*. It is necessary to read Pound's poetry to understand his criticism and to read his criticism to understand his poetry.[3]

My belief in the truth of Eliot's assertion accounts for the inclusion of a discussion of Pound as preceptor in the present book.

The author of *The Waste Land* had good reason to extol Pound's critical acumen, as was revealed in November of 1968 when the unearthing in the New York Public Library vaults of the long-sought-for original manuscript, blue penciled by E.P., was widely publicized. *Time* magazine on that occasion juxtaposed Pound's gifts as a teacher and as a critic by captioning Wyndham Lewis's sketch of him "the ferrule of the teacher."[4] Later, *Time*'s feature writer said of the operations on *The Waste Land:* "A kind of miracle happened: the ferrule of the teacher became the poet's magic wand."[5]

In "Date Line," Pound separates criticism as he conceives it into five categories: (*a*) by discussion, as in Dante's *De Vulgari Eloquentia,* (*b*) by translation, (*c*) by imitation of a style, (*d*) by way of music, as he illustrates in his two operas based on the poets Villon and Cavalcanti, and (*e*) by new composition.[6] He then proceeds to divide its uses into the thought-process immediately prefacing creation (a benefit for artists only) and excernment, an unusual word which might broadly be understood as "seeing into" and in a narrower sense as "editing." The Latinate term derives from a search for a new way of speaking about criticism, for Pound an art meant for sifting out what is most valuable in the recorded *Sagetrieb* ("tale of the tribe"). On a more profound level, criticism, in his view, aims at making some contribution toward a *paideuma,* or culture, by the discovery of relationships among certain literary phenomena, leading to a body of knowledge necessary for the substructure of a cultured society.[7]

Many anthologists of criticism or historians of this branch of literature tend to exclude Pound, perhaps as a result of taking too literally his "Let it stand that the function of criticism is to efface itself when it has established its dissociations." [8] The fact is that these dissociations have to be established again and again if "the tale of the tribe" is to be told in purified, precise, vigorous language. Moreover, certain of Pound's essays, such as "A Few Don'ts for Imagistes," have become classics that no one has any wish to obliterate and that continue to affect the writing of poetry, just as they did at the time of their first publication.

Pound himself has never been much given to reading criticism, partly because of his dislike for abstractions, which inevitably predominate in such writing. Among his personal books, he has kept Eliot's critical essays, since these were the gifts of a friend. Another rather rare sign of interest in the theoretical is his retention of *The Name and Nature of Poetry* by A. E. Housman, which he marked up in the thirties and on which he wrote an article. His co-poets in English, however, both famous and obscure, are well represented in his private collection: Browning, Meredith, Crabbe, Beddoes, Byron, Wordsworth, Denham, the early balladeers, Coleridge,

Armstrong, Dyer, Green, Beattie, Blair, Falconer, Church, Yeats, Moore (Marianne), Joyce, Manning, Eliot, H.D., Bunting, Ford. Most of these names turn up sooner or later in what he wrote, since we usually want to share what we love.

Pound's enthusiasms are so pervasive and so affirmatively proclaimed that a half-century of intellectually curious men and women have followed down the pathways of those interests he has opened up to them. In the preface to his 1910 edition of *The Spirit of Romance* he says: "The history of literature is hero-worship." [9] In addition to the heroes enshrined in *The Cantos,* Pound acquaints the reader of his criticism with such figures as Lucius Apuleius, Saint Francis Bernadone, François Villon, Lope de Vega. Everyone knows of his passion for the twelfth-century Arnaut Daniel, whose *maestria* was praised by Dante in the phrase which Eliot applies to Pound: *il miglior fabbro,* or "the better craftsman." Many of these literary interests he owes to the inspired teacher of his Hamilton days, William P. Shepard, who brought him through the rudiments of French, Italian, Spanish, and Provençal verse of the medieval period. Later the Lope de Vega expert Hugo Rennert, at the University of Pennsylvania, furthered his bent for translation and for critical essays. In the pursuit of his de Vega studies, Pound took all of southern Europe for his classroom and became more qualified each day to act as cicerone through the beginnings of Renaissance literature.

From the winters of 1913 to 1916, when even the great William Butler Yeats looked upon his secretary in the little Sussex stone cottage as preceptor, to the present era of neo-Romantics, Pound's *magisterium* has been revered. Several generations of writers have found in his prose the example of a critic who knows what poems he likes and can tell why in a way that sustains original creative action. For over thirty years he held one "workshop" after another in his various apartments from London to Paris to Rapallo, or he conducted seminars of art theory in the restaurants he frequented in these places. When he retired from the capital of France to the relative obscurity of a small Italian beach town, he continued to be dominated by one passion: "And gladly wolde he lerne, and gladly teche." William Sievert comments on the pedagogy which went on in the Via Marsala of Rapallo:

The "quiet life," however, was frequently disturbed by visits from famous literary and artistic people from all over Europe and, later, by frequent visits from Pound's young followers, for he always was encouraging new talents—he never gave up his role as teacher after he so unceremoniously left Wabash College in Indiana.[10]

Characteristic of his *persona* as preceptor is the text increasingly used by college English classes, *ABC of Reading*, which New Directions made available in paperback in 1960. The subtitle, *Gradus ad Parnassum*, relates it directly to composition: it is principally for the person who desires to ascend as practitioner the mount of the Muses. Moreover, it is for the reader who is receptive, eager to learn, not for those who have arrived at full knowledge of the subject without knowing the facts, as the title page describes pretentiousness in the old. Natural and joyous, Pound's *ABC of Reading* begins in a mood of Mozartian gaiety: "Gloom and solemnity are entirely out of place in even the most rigorous study of an art originally intended to make glad the heart of man." [11] One of the genuinely pivotal books of this century, it lays down a methodology as useful as comparable studies by Eliot.

Taking as a model Pound's own "A Few Don'ts for Imagistes," one might draw up "A Few Do's for Critics" from its pages:

1. Weed out famous but inconsequential writing in order to concentrate on the classics, which never fail to have "a certain and irrepressible freshness." [12]

2. In the spirit of Agassiz, read and compare.

3. Make personal documented statements, in line with the meaning of *criticize* ("to pick out for oneself").[13]

4. Learn to distinguish between "inventors" and "masters."

5. Ground your taste in a thorough knowledge of the best poems, beginning with the oldest in each genre, for example "The Seafarer," where English poetry starts.[14]

The relevance of the last to the composition of Pound's longest work is obvious. Climbing Parnassus requires an apprenticeship in taste to "the singing masters of the soul" who have gone before. Such acquaintance is necessary not only for reasons of technique but also, as *The Cantos* reveals from its outset, in order to supply material for incorporation into the poetry itself. No one has so well demonstrated as Pound the fragmentary nature of contemporary consciousness. He has gone fishing amidst masterpieces and dumped his glittering catch into the net of his writing, where in the very first Canto (the *Nekuia*) "The Seafarer" jostles the *Odyssey*. To perceive this dependence on the past is to understand what Pound meant by quoting his own discarded lines as headnote to the recent "guidebook" to *The Cantos:* "Say that I dump my catch, shiny and silvery/ As fresh sardines slapping and slipping on the marginal cobbles." [15]

His earlier annotated book list, *How to Read,* Pound judges too polemical to serve in the classroom. However, like the *ABC of Reading,* it is important for its evaluations and definitions. To Allanah Harper he confides that *How to Read* is the outcome of his twenty-five-year struggle to learn something about comparative literature.[16] Fascinating as the volume is, it is in no sense a text.

The second section of the *ABC of Reading* (about a hundred pages) is given over to "exhibits," reaching down in time as far as Whitman in America and Browning in England. Pound accompanies each selection with witty, condensed, casual notes. It is hard to imagine this Baedeker for scholars as having been written so many years ago, so contemporary is its tone. In this last part of the book, passages from the sixteenth-century Mark Alexander Boyd and the seventeenth-century Earl of Dorset resemble the obscurities unearthed by Yvor Winters. Pound calls the citation from Boyd "the most beautiful sonnet in the language"; [17] unless one is an expert in Scottish dialect it is difficult to refute him, especially since he may have meant the superlative praise as restricted to works in Boyd's dialect and not to sonnets in the larger tongue, English. Undeniably, the picture of Cupid and his mother, Venus, is lovely, the goddess "a wife ingenuit of the sea/ And lichter nor a dauphin with her fin." Were the comparison to embrace all of English sonnets, Pound's own "A Virginal" has a rather good chance for the distinction which he cavalierly awards to Mark Boyd.

The book ends with a treatise on meter. Those who wish to learn about this topic from Pound go first, quite naturally, to his poetic achievement: hundreds of metrical subtleties abound in each of the Cantos. Yet the principles laid down here can help one to profit from his practice. They belong to the "preaching to the mob" which occupied the happiest years of his career, a maturity which brought together criticism and poem-making in a fertile interchange. The saying of Saint Francis "We have only so much learning as we put into action" always informs Pound's approach, so that he is never merely theorist.

That the poet conceived of himself as preceptor is clear from that essay of his, in Eliot's culling, entitled "The Teacher's Mission." He envisions this mission as a restoration of language from its corruption through journalism, in order that the "HEALTH OF THE NATIONAL MIND" be maintained.[18] No one can achieve success as a teacher unless he first examine his own interior condition—a flashback to Confucius—and then turn toward the light in all openness. In the study of poetry Pound desires, as the furthest possible remove from abstraction, a comparison of masterpieces. This method rests upon disciplined concreteness such as is found in the ideogram's union of word and thing. Administrators should instruct rather than suppress teachers who they feel err. A Franciscan emphasis emanates from sentences like "Education that does not bear on LIFE and on the most vital and immediate problems of the day is not education but merely suffocation and sabotage." [19]

Accuracy for Pound is a goal consistently held to. In art its corresponding value would be that merit which he believes

Jacob Epstein demonstrates in his birds in stone or metal:
"They have that greatest quality of art, to wit: certitude." [20]
His demolition of "beaneries" through invective in letter,
essay, or conversation can be interpreted not as negativism or
rancor but rather as a passion for exactness such as one might
expect to find in a *Quattrocento* studio or in the laboratory of
Louis Agassiz. Whole books like *Jefferson and/or Mussolini*
are written in a caustic spirit, to goad readers into making
distinctions. At least five Cantos enshrine his love for conciseness in their employment of the *ching ming* ideogram, which
might well serve as emblem for the intent of all his critical
prose.

In addition to the above-mentioned account of metrics
which concludes the *ABC of Reading*, some of Pound's best
statements on prosody occur in his memoirs of the artist
Gaudier-Brzeska, whose notebooks are among his most prized
keepsakes. It is here that he speaks of an absolute rhythm as
existing for every emotion; [21] of images as having a variable significance, like *a* and *b* and *c* in algebra; [22] of the image as the
poet's pigment,[23] "the word beyond formulated language," [24]
the "radiant node or cluster through which ideas are rush-
ing." [25] In its pages he comments on how colors match certain emotions,[26] reemphasizing his fear of abstractions.[27]
In a *dictum* recalling Plato he calls harmony the meeting
place of the arts.[28]

Most hostile critics accuse Pound of violating the adage
"Shoemaker, stick to your last" because his essays often range
far from literature. However, a man lives his life as he
chooses: style includes, among other things, the subjects one
elects to write about. From at least his forties on, the lion's
share of Pound's energies went into economics. It is not ex-

traordinary that an artist whose penury—as did Hart Crane's —forced him to battle to make a living should seize upon money, its nature and distribution, as an *idée fixe*. Pound had been brought up on family stories of that pioneer in currency reform, his grandfather Thaddeus C. Pound. Moreover, he was accustomed to visit the glimmering storehouses of silver, gold, and bronze coins at the Philadelphia Mint, where Homer Loomis Pound worked. He early felt the image value of this subject. As an adult, sharp need of money for his dependents as well as for himself caused him to focus more and more on the roots of inequality in a world sufficiently endowed with goods for all men to live a decent life free from painful worry.

In *Vision Fugitive: Ezra Pound and Economics*, Earle Davis has traced the development of Pound's economic theories as these affected his verse and has fitted into their proper place the economists Veblen, Fisher, Douglas, Gesell, del Mar, Kitson, and the others whom Pound unceasingly urged his pupils to absorb. Believing that the Church, which for many centuries had stood firmly for the right use of money, had abandoned its integrity when it permitted usury, he not only stormed and preached but wrote some of the most exquisite poetry of his Cantos on this subject: the two on *usura*. Widely depreciated as his theories are, even someone as divergent from him as William Carlos Williams came to accept Pound's position on usury in his epic *Paterson*.

Pound's curriculum is not always to the liking even of those students most sympathetic to him, as Davis notes:

His voyage, like that of Odysseus, has taken him over strange oceans to hell and back. Some of us have had to row madly to keep him in sight. Some of us wish he had occasionally gone in different directions or had listened to Tiresias. But there he is, the beard sticking out at an angle, the eyes flashing with the light of other worlds, the anchor of Social Credit pulled up safely inside the boat, his rudder set for Ithaca or what he imagines to be paradise.[29]

If one is to comprehend the last fourth of the Cantos, he will be forced to learn at least the outline of a history of money, some familiarity with which is needed in order to make any sense of them at all. Realizing how such a requirement will alienate readers, Pound nevertheless thinks the issue important enough to take that risk.

From those days in Venice, when he lived largely on barley soup in the *trattorie* of San Gregorio, to the Rome or Rapallo diatribes against monetary abuses as the source of wars and other public evils, Pound advanced from an experiential student of poverty into the professor's chair. He never forgot his "laboratory" realization of what it meant to be poor. Unable to agree with men who, like Arthur Griffiths, failed to see economics as a force capable of eliciting an emotional as well as an intellectual reaction, he gave his voice, as well as pen, pencil, or typewriter, both on the Italian Riviera and during those last incarcerated years in America, to educating those who would listen or read.

Pound has ever been quick to commend those few academic preceptors whom he regards as outstanding. At Saint Elizabeth's in the 1950s, he wrote with warm remembrance to a favorite elementary-school instructor, Florence Ridpath, by that time retired to a Methodist home in Philadelphia. He describes her to Carl Gatter: "She was a teacher the kids liked, and that, I suppose, ran counter to the efficiency mania for crushing humanity out of existence." [30] From Italy earlier he had written an expression of condolence to Professor Roy F. Nichols and the rest of the University of Pennsylvania history department when a colleague of theirs died suddenly:

The idea that a student might have a legitimate curiosity was in no way alien to his [Dr. Ames's] sensibilities. All of which goes into the making of a strong personal affection lasting over three decades with no more nutriment than perhaps two or three letters. [31]

That very February Pound had sent Professor Ames a letter, though it arrived after the death. *The Cantos,* as well as correspondence, testifies that Doolittle, Shepard, Schelling, Rennert were not forgotten by their pupil. Yet though he could praise, he could be scathing where he saw mediocrity, a failure of imagination, or pomposity.

Originally, it had been Pound's intention to devote his own life to teaching, and, as William Sievert affirms, in a broad sense he has done so:

By this time [1908], he had earned his Master of Arts degree from the University; he was ready to begin a career which in one way or another he would continue for the rest of his life; the career was that of teacher. [32]

Eliot, writing in *The Literary Essays of Ezra Pound,* says: "He has always been, first and foremost, a teacher and campaigner." [33] Dedicated to Basil Bunting and Louis Zukofsky, *Guide to Kulchur* shows him in this light. It is based upon the theme which Clark Emery used for the title of his volume on Pound, *Ideas into Action.* In Emery's words, "The history of a culture is the history of ideas going into action." [34] If Pound infuriates with his rock-drill persistence,

he does so designedly. Having no personal interest to advance, but merely the cause of truth as he sees it, he romps
about in iconoclastic glee easily mistaken for temper. He is
serious in the manner that Molière and Jonson are serious.
Under his sometimes heavy-handed wit runs the desire for
betterment which he believes should animate the critic, who
is no idle smeller of roses but a fierce enemy of stupidity and
ignorance, close companions though not identical twins. Both
criticism and poetry to Pound are didactic, an epithet he
would acknowledge as unashamedly as Dante. Education he
has called the art of making distinctions, an art in which
Pound excels whether in prose or in poetry. One example is
his gift for definition, as in "Art is a fluid moving above or
over the minds of men." [35] In *The Spirit of Romance* he says
quite frankly: "The aim of the present work is to instruct. Its
ambition is to instruct painlessly." [36] His essays do just that,
whereas the instruction effected by his verse, since its wisdom
is harder to "earn," may not always be painless.

In such prose works as *Guide to Kulchur*, Pound reveals
the breadth of his reading, just as the canon of his works reveals the scope of his tremendous creative talents. Where
among today's writers can we find one who has investigated
more thoroughly Stevenson's "The world is so full of a number of things"? He is indeed a reconstruction of the Renaissance "complete man" (*polumetis*). Like Mauberley, he seems
to have been born out of his age—to be, in fact, a composite
of several ages. Music, painting, sculpture, as well as literature, fall under his scrutiny. The *Quattrocento* would have
been a natural milieu for him: "The fifteenth century is,
above all, that of the many-sided man. There is no biography

that does not, besides the chief work of its hero, speak of other pursuits, all of which pass beyond mere dilettantism." [37] Lyrics, letters, plays, translations, operas—in all he excels, just as he is at home in every century and on every continent.

Pound's latest critical thought lies in his notes to *Confucius to Cummings: An Anthology of Poetry,* compiled with Marcella Spann, now a young English teacher in a Connecticut college and in a position to carry out her preceptor's theories as well as to promulgate his preferences in literature. Containing almost a hundred selections, the book is meant for the reader who knows only English. It might be considered a second-semester text, to follow the *ABC of Reading.* As indicated in the title, the anthology commences with the sixth-century B.C. Chinese sage, out of whose writings Pound picks a poem called "Confucius," which he annotates with the words "Here the actual author speaks." [38] Out of line with the stance on voice and address of the influential *Understanding Poetry,* edited by Cleanth Brooks and Robert Penn Warren, he qualifies by stating that "I" and the poet are one, since after all the piece is a dramatic monologue: the same fusion, contrary to the thesis of this text, holds true again and again in autobiographical sequences of *The Cantos,* though recognition of this identity is slow in coming.

All Pound scholars approach this book with curiosity about its inclusions from among the entire spectrum of world literature. Homer, of course, they expect to find present, and he is. Among all the available translations, it is to George Chapman that Pound turns here for a poetic rendition, possibly because, except for Alexander Pope, he was the greatest writer (outside of Pound himself) to attempt the translation of the

Odyssey. If his choice among versions of Aeschylus is puzzling, it may be that he settled on Dallas Simpson's Negro-dialect opening of the *Agamemnon* to serve as a spoof on those who take their classics too solemnly, a danger pointed out in the *ABC of Reading*. In the medieval section, there appears Pound's own translation of Saint Francis's "Cantico del Sole, [39] little known although it is probably the very best version to date.

In the third Appendix, Pound sets down three questions that any teacher using this text should first ask himself and then propose to his students:

(a) Why is the poem included in the anthology?
(b) What moved the author to write it?
(c) What does it tell the reader? [40]

These three points are crucial in that they constitute an approach based on affirmative reactions, always far more productive of helpful criticism than fault-finding, as Pound implies in paraphrasing his former English teacher Felix Schelling.[41] In this collection he remarks, as he has elsewhere, that only from the artist will notable criticism come.[42] Hardly an incontrovertible view, it is nevertheless his position, and he maintains it.

Within the texture of Pound's chef d'oeuvre, critical insights of his own or in reported talk appear from time to time as evidences of the civilized man's concern about language. In Canto 80 he writes: "To communicate and then stop, that is the law of discourse," rephrasing the adage in Canto 87 as "Get the meaning across and then quit." These sentences go far toward explaining his silence of recent years, so bewildering to those used to his ebullient youth and middle age. The ideogram *chih*,[3] "to stop or desist," occurs in Canto 52 for the first time, bearing the same significance as these two maxims above; Canto 60 expands it:

> He ordered 'em to prepare a total anatomy, et
> qu'ils veillèrent à la pureté du langage
> et qu'on n'employât que de termes propres
> (namely CH'ing ming)

A half-dozen Cantos incorporate this ideogram, even as late as Canto 110, wherein Pound uses it twice. In Canto 77 it takes the form of "the precise definition," a crystallization of his Imagist tenet, in fact the height toward which the Cantos in their rising sweep endlessly strive.

Though *The Cantos* is the essential Pound, his prose works soar far above journalism and have had enormous impact in promoting the enjoyment of a myriad of heretofore unknown literary personages, besides directing the talents of his younger contemporaries. Not only are they pleasurable reading for their own sake but they are indispensable for the light they throw on the poetry.

CHAPTER 3

Pound's Early Lyrics

Pound's first published book (1908) had the rather melancholy title *A Lume Spento*,[1] chosen to reflect the mourning he felt for his friend William Brooke Smith, to whom it was dedicated ("And Mt. Taishan is faint as the wraith of my first friend/ who comes talking ceramics," Canto 77). Each of his early volumes is in its own way a portrait of the artist as a young man, not Ezra Loomis Pound from Hailey, Idaho, and Wyncote, Pennsylvania, but an etherealized *persona*.

Fairly often the pieces call up in the memory some phrase or locale or topic developed by Eliot. This resemblance may have sprung from a common influence or have been Pound's own idiom, later borrowed from by Eliot. Such a likeness is seen in "Erat Hora":

> "Thank you, whatever comes." And then she turned
> And, as the ray of sun on hanging flowers
> Fades when the wind hath lifted them aside,
> Went swiftly from me. Nay, whatever comes
> One hour was sunlit and the most high gods
> May not make boast of any better thing
> Than to have watched that hour as it passed.

The imagery of this poem clearly suggests "La Figlia Che Piange." We know that we are *in medias res* from the four words spoken by the lady, "Thank you, whatever comes." In a similar way the Eliot lyric places us momentarily in the midst of a love affair, though the thought of it later brings torment rather than peace: the participant in "Erat Hora" is so caught up in the bliss of the sun-drenched hour that he considers the vision of it a lovelier paradise than the very gods themselves enjoy.

In certain passages this juvenile celebration of an hour shows an ability to work with language as men actually speak it in conversation or record it in letters, the sort of writing which Yeats little by little learned to employ. But its author cannot entirely put away the Romanticism to which an archaic *hath* comes more readily than *has*. The wind rustling through the vine-blossoms of the farewell setting, unlike the scrap of dialogue, follows the poetic custom of the day by taking the nineteenth-century, or earlier, auxiliary verb. In "Nay, whatever comes/ One hour was sunlit," the omission of *Nay* would have created an effective silence between the two halves of the line. Compensatory for this lapse is the making of *hour* into a two-syllabled word in "Than to have watched that hour as it passed," a rather admirable little success in duration. The somewhat pretentious Latin title, a characteristic device of this period, reveals Pound's lack of self-criticism at the time, as does the superfluous *Nay*.

To see how steadily Pound was advancing in technique one need only compare "Erat Hora" with another good-bye, that of Canto 4 (he had been composing *The Cantos* even before the appearance of *A Lume Spento*). Herein is presented as a fragment of a drama the 'suicide of a thirteenth-century *donna* who discovers she has eaten her lover's heart through a trick perpetrated by the malice of a jealous husband:

> And she went toward the window,
> > the slim white stone bar
> Making a double arch;
> Firm even fingers held to the firm pale stone;
> Swung for a moment,
> > and the wind out of Rhodez
> Caught in the full of her sleeve.
> > . . . the swallows crying:

Perhaps this incident never happened, as Robert S. Briffault asserts: "The details of this [the troubadour Guilhem de Cabestanh's] life are overshadowed by the poetic legend with which his name is associated; an incensed husband killed him, it is said, and gave his wife her lover's heart to eat." [2] So convincing is Pound's rendition, however, that it is almost impossible to believe that the tragedy did not occur in just the way pictured.

A poem more effective than "Erat Hora" and on the same theme is "A Virginal," with its unforgettable opening: "No, no! Go from me. I have left her lately./ I will not spoil my sheath with lesser brightness. . . ." Many early Pound lyrics were intended for musical accompaniment; this definitely was, as the title indicates. "A Virginal" represents an advance in sophistication of meter, especially its trochaic line-beginnings: "Slight are her arms," "Soft as spring wind," and "Green come the shoots." It is as perfect as anything in Thomas Campion. Those who find Pound confusing can well contemplate the orderliness with which he here builds his litany of similes. Keeping to the rhyme scheme of the English sonnet, he intensifies with each comparison the impression of his lady's delicacy. Probably the best touch, apart from the introduction, is the image of April staunching winter's wound with her sleight hand. The succinct tributes are unified by their background: a birch grove, fragrant and white in the youth of the year. No *donna ideale* of the Provençal minstrels is more beautiful than this all-but-divine ethereal creature.

Sometimes the extravagances of setting in *A Lume Spento* remind us of the tales of Edgar Allan Poe, minus the verisimilitude which Poe strives for in his pseudo-medieval interiors. The "six great sapphires" on the wall, level with the heroine's knees in "The House of Splendour," seem straight out of Poe, as do the many rooms of gold, patterned in enamel and "beaten work," with "aureate light" streaming through claret windows. In this lyric the speaker might be relating a dream about his mistress Evanoe and her house, which, like the Christian Heavenly City, is "not made with hands." The building appears more a shining cobweb than a mansion: "Her gold is spread, above, around, inwoven; / Strange ways and walls are fashioned out of it." Pound has adopted the British spelling of *splendour,* as is his custom with such words. He derives the woman's name from his study of Romance languages: stemming from the Latin *evanescere* (to vanish), the adjective *evanescent* is defined in *Webster's New International Dictionary,* Third Edition, as fleeting, fragile, diaphanous, the last meaning being illustrated with a quotation from the *New Republic* in such a way as to connect the word with Pound's heroine ("with the evanescent brushwork and psychological clarity since lost in English painting").

In the *ABC of Reading* Pound states the foundation of his

prosody: "Rhythm is a form cut into TIME, as a design is determined SPACE." [3] Two lines from "The House of Splendour" are triumphs of cadence, felt even if elusive in discussion: "And I have seen my Lady in the sun"; "And red the sunlight was behind it all." The description of Evanoe's hair as "a sheaf of wings" has more affinity to Pre-Raphaelitism than to Louis Agassiz (later Pound's model for accuracy of observation) or to Botticelli. If readers find this metaphor vague, hard to visualize, they must remember that Pound was going through his own Celtic Twilight. Another Yeatsian passage is line three, "But out somewhere beyond the worldly ways." On the whole, such examples of juvenilia do not bear signs of having undergone any extensive revision.

The diction of "The House of Splendour" (*'Tis, a-level, am* instead of *have, perforce, Behold, mine, Maketh*) continues the obsolescence dominant in "Erat Hora." The weakest aspect of the Evanoe lyric is its verbiage. Yet to compare Pound in his twenties with Pound the mature poet is only to enhance remarkably the latter. Moreover, in "The House of Splendour" the effect sought is the indistinctness of a dream, one akin to the tremulousness of the woven branches above the ocean strands of Yeats's "The Man Who Dreamed of Faeryland." Conceiving of it in this way renders the poem more magical in the culminating lines:

> and there are powers in this
> Which, played on by the virtues of her soul,
> Break down the four-square walls of standing time.

Up to the concluding verse, one has been listening to the improvisations of Peter Quince at his clavier and letting the music of Evanoe dissolve the barriers of sense. Then suddenly one is confronted with what is a central intention of *The Cantos:* the penetration of the world of phenomena into the eternal.

Classifiable among the same "vision" poetry as "The House of Splendour" is "Apparuit." One is distracted by the abhorrence with which the older artist would have regarded "carven in subtle stuff," so contrary to his later "medallion" manner, or intaglio style, aimed at fineness of outline. Yet one should not look too closely at a phantom, and somehow the six stanzas create what is implied in the translation of the title, "She appears." Anglo-Saxon metrical strength takes over as each of the quatrains ends in a dactyl and trochee, their vigorous downbeats threatening the Burne-Jones mood of the entire composition. The poem seems actually to be made of light: "Golden rose," the flickering lamp, "the glamorous sun," the golden tissue clothing the lady, her "shell of gold." The images reach a climax in three heavy accents: "the stunned light/ faded about thee." Such a line invites a pause wherein to savor the exquisite character of the central personification. The illusion of intangible gold continues as the woman's throat is seen to be scarved in light. Echoing Ernest Dawson, Pound uses "gone as wind" to express the exit of his beloved as she departs in "goldish weft." One is grateful to critic Thomas H. Jackson for pointing out that the *Vita Nuova* introduces Beatrice in the words *Apparuit jam beatitudo vestra* (II, 31).[4] The heroine of the Dantean epic which Pound as a Hamilton undergraduate learned to read in the Italian may possibly be the figure referred to here, though she might also be any similar source of man's (or a man's) happiness.

"Erat Hora," "The House of Splendour," "Apparuit" belong

to dreamscape; the youthful Ezra, however, had other than "mystic" strings to his bow. "Portrait d'une Femme" could just as well have been written by Eliot. Both men take this title for poems about a no-longer-young woman who is famous as a hostess. The rather illogical opening of Pound's ("Your mind and you are our Sargasso Sea") is quite different from the precision of riper stages in his career, but already the conversational approach which he encouraged in Yeats is beginning to emerge: "You have been second always. Tragical?/ No. You preferred it to the usual thing." This type of idiom is one of the virtues Herbert Schneidau very likely has in mind when he praises this poem as forecasting the writer's mature style.[5] A search for the exact word, as in Flaubert, had not as yet absorbed Pound's energies. The thrice-employed *strange* would have seemed less an inartistic repetition had he inserted another word before the *gain* or the *woods* which it modifies. Basically in iambic pentameter, "Portrait d'une Femme" acquires more interest through the presence of juxtaposed accents: "Strange woods half sodden and new brighter stuff." Here the alliterative arrangement is another throwback to Anglo-Saxon. This woman whose social existence depends upon relaying bits of talk from one guest to the next reminds one of a Jamesian character, though the Master would have selected and combined words so that none was unnecessary.

The treasures which the real Sargasso Sea captures in its gulfweed from the wrecks of ships include "Idols and ambergris and rare inlays." In parody, this gossiper's riches are described as a "sea-hoard of things deciduous," the last term chosen for its secondary sense of *ephemeral, transitory*. Somehow, the imagination has a hard time in fusing this metaphor of transience with the permanence of idols and precious inlaid art-objects. Yet Pound, in a single line, cannot help revealing the true poet that he is: "In the slow float of different light and deep." This epithet for light recalls Matthew Arnold's employment of *various* in "Dover Beach" and raises the passage to "memorable speech," as Auden defines poetry. Occasional internal and end-rhymes, plus repetition, tighten the sketch, setting it to a Jacobean music. No line approximates the accentual pattern of any other. The poem resembles in subject "The Garden," which pictures an equally sterile though more isolated woman as she faces the diminishments of growing older.

Of Pound's two poems on the dance, "The Return" and "Dance Figure," the second has perhaps not been praised to the degree that it merits. "The Return," from the 1912 *Ripostes,* shows him more intent on his combinations of sound than in what he is saying. Over half of the twenty lines begin with a forceful downbeat, like the taps of feet performing some solemn ritual. The sense of this poem has a Georgian vagueness about it not inappropriate for a drama whose actors are revenants. As the allusions become more definite, oddly enough they grow more confused, until one has a choric group of figures who resemble Hermes, with silver hounds accompanying them; in a sudden shift to the past tense they turn out to be no more than weak shadowy beings out of the Erebus decried by Achilles in the *Iliad.* "The Return" is the nearest Pound comes to Symbolism as practiced by Mallarmé; this literary movement was a siren which did not detain him long, as it did his younger contemporary Hart

Crane. Even with the assistance of Canto 1, the translation of the Homeric descent to hell, one scarcely knows how to interpret the "souls of blood" or ghost-hounds. The lines "Slow on the leash,/ pallid the leash-men!" which appear as a concluding couplet are a troubadour's *envoi,* written for no other reason than to parallel the late-medieval form.

Examined from another angle, "The Return" is an example of the Vorticist code. Why need verbal designs correspond any more closely to "the way things are" than the Cubistic fantasies of Duchamp, or the Wyndham Lewises to which Pound remained consistently loyal? In the essay "Vorticism" he says: "Secondly, I made poems like 'The Return,' which is an objective reality and has a complicated sort of significance, like Mr. Epstein's 'Sun God,' or Mr. Brzeska's 'Boy with a Coney'." [6] The cross-movement of "The Return"—the dead seeking earth, the snow seeking the sky—manipulates the durations of syllables until Pound has achieved that integrity which is one property of beauty. Were there no other cause for admiration, the comparison of dancers to snowflakes hesitating in the wind, half turning back, would give the poem aesthetic value.

The second of the dance songs, "Dance Figure," which came out in the 1916 *Lustra,* is grounded in reality rather than in the imaginary by its subtitle "For the Marriage in Cana of Galilee." Yet the Palestinian theme has more in common with Joyce's "Araby" and Stevens's "Sunday Morning" than with the New Testament record of the celebration in Galilee. The queen of the dancers has little about her of Judaic culture, except the connotations of "the well-head" and its "women with pitchers." The feet here are as swift as they were slow in "The Return": no winged shoes aid these mortal dancers in their ivory sandals. In "The Ballad of the Goodly Fere" Pound stays close to the spirit and details of the Gospel, but in "Dance Figure" he creates a setting of Oriental luxury, complete with eunuchs, bars of copper, beds of gilt turquoise and silver—hardly the house of a neighbor of Mary of Nazareth. The leading performer, "Tree-at-the-river," is described part by part as in the Song of Songs—arms like the flesh under the bark of a young sapling, face like a river whereon drift lighted boats, hands like a streamlet through the sedge, fingers fluid as a brook after frost. Pound attains a climactic effect in his line "A brown robe, with threads of gold woven in patterns, has thou gathered about thee." This image foreshadows the famous Canto passage: "In the gloom the gold gathers the light about it." The dark-eyed beauty, accompanied by her maidens that are like white pebbles, represents a lady of his dreams closer to a trouvère ideal than to the Blessed Virgin or one of her companions. The presence of a refrain characteristic of Provençal song indicates Pound's intent to imitate Ventadorn, Daniel, and their fellows: "There is none like thee among the dancers;/ None with swift feet."

These two songs on dancers illustrate exactly the view of poetic art elucidated in *Polite Essays:*

Dante has defined a poem as a composition of words set to music, and the intelligent critic will demand that either the composition of words or the music shall possess a certain interest, or that there be some aptitude in their being joined together.[7]

The pair are composed of words such as one might sing to the strumming of a stringed instrument, with an accent at intervals from a triangle. Nonrepresentational figures seem as justifiable as the pure sounds of music. That Pound was intrigued with abstract art as a model for poetry is obvious from his lyric "A Game of Chess," with its analogues in Braque, Gris, Picasso, other painters. Babette Deutsch elaborates on the Duchamp-like title: "This poem, we are told, is a 'Dogmatic Statement Concerning the Game of Chess: Theme for a Series of Pictures,' and indeed it summons up for the mind's eye a fine example of cubism."[8]

Though ridiculed by its writer, "The Ballad of the Goodly Fere" won Pound a wide readership. It is subtitled "Simon Zelotes speaketh it somewhile after the Crucifixion." The form, dramatic monologue, is no new one to him ("Cino" is an example), but to confine it to ballad meter was an innovation. Not always does Pound keep within the *persona* of the rough fisherman Peter, who is telling the tale. Most conspicuously does he lapse in "The hounds of the crimson sky gave tongue/ But never a cry cried he."

Pound strives for a dialect impression by omitting a letter here and there, as in *o'* for *of*, and by using the archaisms *twey, aye, ye, drave*. While keeping to the 4/3 accent pattern, he secures variation by the addition of so many unaccented syllables that a line of perfect iambic ("His smile was good to see") is rare. A first reading fails to reveal all the technique which has gone into this anthology piece. The verses are linked together by twenty-seven end-rhymes, many of them identical: *tree, sea, see, he, free, he, company, he, free, treasury, cunningly, sea, degree, tree, he, tree, be, tree, free, he, Galilee, sea, free, suddenly, sea, eternally, tree*—the sort of thing Arnaut Daniel would have reveled in. Alliteration, vocabulary, and caesura relate the piece, like the others scrutinized, to his favorite Anglo-Saxon tradition (e.g., *fere* as meaning companion).

The major image in the poem is the sea: Christ as the lover of "ships and the open sea"; Christ with "his eyes like the grey o' the sea":

> Like the sea that brooks no voyaging
> With the winds unleashed and free,
> Like the sea that he cowed at Genseret
> Wi' twey words spoke suddenly.

This Jesus is brother to Bertran de Born, troubadour, in "Sestina: Altaforte," which, like "Near Perigord," elaborates the belligerence of the war-lord whom Dante's *Inferno* condemns for the sowing of discord but who belongs to a type of leader —few, thank God, if perhaps necessary—who lifts the mediocrity of life to a heroic crest. Christ is not only "mate of the wind and sea" but commander of the thundering heavens rent with lightning which roofed the arena of his going forth.

Pound's boyhood had been Presbyterian, his church attendance regular. Not until he had flown from the nest did he cease affiliating with a definite sect of worshippers. His juvenilia on the Magi, Angels, the Virgin Mary, the Nativity mystery he has chosen not to retain in circulation. The 1963 volume of *Current Biography* quotes him as saying humorously about this popular monologue of Simon's: "All I had to do was to write a ballad about each of the disciples and I would have been set for life." [9] The truth probably was that he grew as tired of hearing "The Ballad of the Goodly Fere" recited as Yeats did "The Lake Isle of Innisfree." Subjective reactions such as these, even those of their authors, cannot tarnish the worth of the lyrics involved.

Much the same orthodox concept of the Deity prevails in "Ballad for Gloom," beginning "For God, our God is a gallant foe/ That playeth behind the veil." Its theme is that to lose to God is actually to win. "Night Litany" is by far the strongest and loveliest of Pound's theistic poems from this period profoundly influenced by Christian dogma. Superb in its nocturnal description, the lyric deserves Miss Deutsch's comment that it is to the canals of Venice what "The Seafarer" is to the savage seas of the Vikings.[10] "Night Litany" serves well as an introduction of high school students to Pound, just as "The Ballad of Father Gilligan" does to Yeats. Its omission from the New Directions *Selected Poems* and from most collections of American literature is to be regretted.

Other evidences of Pound's Wyncote religious background apppear in the jaunty "Villonaud for This Yule," a discarded verse-dialogue commemorating the Bethlehem story. Its second line is a rather nebulous prayer: "Christ make the shepherds' homage dear!" The Wise Men enter the tableau in the second stanza, although in an interrogative mode, rather than the imperative one of the opening petition. In Pound's context, these Magi are actors in a ghost sonata. By the third stanza, Christian imagery has been replaced by Saturn, Mars, and Zeus as Nativity horoscope symbols. Each of the three stanzas of eight tetrameter verses closes with a witty echo of François Villon's most famous refrain: "Wining the ghosts of yester-year." In Pound's virelay, the two rhymes used exclusively in the first stanza return in the next two, keeping all twenty-four lines to a strict patterning. The *envoi* brings the

poem effectively to an end in the mode of Provençal craftsmanship.

The diction and word-order of the lyric are unnatural, in-
adequacies of which Pound was well aware when from San
Ambrogio at Rapallo he wrote the headnote for a 1965 New
Directions edition of *A Lume Spento and Other Early Poems:*
"As to why a reprint? No lessons to be learned save the depth
of ignorance, or rather the superficiality of non-perception—
neither eye nor ear."

Continuing the series of tributes to the vagabond-king introduced to the poet at Hamilton by Professor Shepard is "A
Villonaud Ballad of the Gibbet, Or the Song of the Sixth
Companion." One of François's prison-mates, under the sentence of death, is the speaker. The syntax of "Drink we a
skoal for the gallows tree," thrice repeated, impresses the
reader as better technique than anything else in this second
Christmas poem "after" Villon. Here the chief religious allu-
sion is to Hell, the negativism canceled out by the convict's
trust in Divine mercy. Pound detects the same compassion in
the fifteenth-century poet that caused Truman Capote to
draw upon the "hanged men" ballad as headnote for *In Cold
Blood.* In spite of obsolescent vocabulary, two lines in
Pound's poem rising from real faith possess a power to move
the heart: "These that we loved shall God love less/ And
smite alway at their faibleness?"

Pound's regard for Villon has endured. The outstanding
testimony is his opera *The Testament of François Villon,* per-
formed by the British Broadcasting Company in 1931, again
in the sixties at Spoleto, and in Berkeley, California, November 13, 1971. Undoubtedly, the work is destined for more pro-

ductions. Joan Fitzgerald, an American-born sculptor who has made her home in Venice, has wrought a life-size bronze statue of François Villon, calling it "Homage to Ezra Pound." The piece catches well the "immortal concept" moving through its incarnations down the centuries. It is hard to conceive of the short-lived French minstrel, that dancing light who was half-flame, half-sword, as passing the fourscore and ten years Biblically allotted to men. Yet who shall say that of all the masks Pound has worn this one is not nearest the center?

Many of the titles in the original *A Lume Spento* have dropped from print, being known today only to specialists. These include "Grace Before Song," "La Fraisne" (retaining interest because spoken by troubadour Peire Vidal), "In Epitaphium Eius," "Mesmerism" (which calls Browning "Old Hippety-Hop of the accents"). "Anima Sola" (note again the penchant for Latin titles) is significant because of its epigraph by Empedokles, part of the Sophoclean age that Pound was to revivify by his genius as translator; it shows how even in his early twenties the metaphor of the crystal sphere attracted him: "Then neither is the bright orb of the sun greeted nor yet either the shaggy might of earth or sea, thus then, in the firm vessel of harmony is fixed God, a sphere, round, rejoicing in complete solitude." Later, he was to use this ball-of-light image to hold together *The Cantos*. In the lyric proper, the only relevant line is "The blood of light is God's delight." In a similar apocalyptic vein, "Beddoesque" calls the crystal sphere "The great whole liquid jewel of God's truth," while "Sandalphon" presents it as "the multiplex jewel of beryl and jasper and sapphire," inspiring the soul to adoration. All

these references, intertwining to a blaze as bright as a holo-
caust, might be considered Homeric omens, foreshadowing
the luminescent "pearl beyond price" which is as unifying in
its own fashion as Whitman's grass-symbol.

The esoteric thought behind "Historion" seems an anticipa-
tion of Yeats's *A Vision*, as yet unwritten. In their turn, souls
of the great pass through Pound's own soul (Dante, Villon,
the saints), their locus "a sphere/ Translucent, molten gold,
that is the 'I.'" Metrically, "This for an instant and the flame
is gone" is the best line among the unrhymed stanzas. It foreshadows the transfiguration in *The Cantos* each time an
Aphrodite sequence breaks through from eternal into tem-
poral order.

One of the chief reasons to return to Ezra Pound's imma-
ture lyrics is to discern therein "seeds" which will reach frui-
tion in *The Cantos*. Native to the imagery of myth in the epic
is "The Spring," with its pageant which

> Through this sylvan place
> Spreads the bright tips,
> And every vine-stock is
> Clad in new brilliancies.

The poem concludes with "Moves only now a clinging
tenuous ghost," an arrangement of words which would never
have been allowed by an older and more fastidious Pound,
who would have recognized that *only* belongs after, not before, *now*. Yet notwithstanding its flaws, the lyric, like others
of the early period, has a mysterious attraction. These tapers
remain unquenched.

Since Eliot is generally considered the arbiter of taste for the first half of this century, it is enlightening to observe what he discarded or added when he edited the *Selected Poems* of Pound in 1927, winnowing from *Personae*, issued the year before. Omitted were "Mr. Housman's Message," "Translations and Adaptations from Heine," "Au Salon," "Au Jardin," "Silet," "In Exitum Cuiusdam," "Les Millwin," "Tempora," "The Bellaires," "The New Cake of Soap," "To Formianus' Young Lady Friend," "Au Contemporaries," "Cantico del Sole," and all six poems from the short-lived periodical *Blast*. Not one of these is any "adjunct to the Muses' diadem." Twenty-six pages of the slender book are devoted to "Homage to Sextus Propertius." In his introduction, Eliot explains why he prefers this adaptation: "One of Pound's most indubitable claims to genuine originality is, I believe, his revivification of the Provençal and the early Italian poetry." [11] By analogy, Pound, in "Propertius" too, made poems so new in turning them from one language to another that the result in each case was a fresh lyric deserving to be grouped under *Selected Poems*.

The longest and most frequently read of Pound's early works is "Hugh Selwyn Mauberley," a rejection of England even though it was a London press that saw fit to publish it in 1920. This Jamesian experiment tells the story of a young expatriate from "a half savage country," who, like Miniver Cheevy, is an anachronism in his native milieu.[12] He is a young author who comes to England, where for three years he struggles against the grain. From the start, he is doomed (as Winterbourne says of himself in *Daisy Miller*) to make a mistake. Mauberley's error is in thinking that he can bring the dead to life. Grounded (consciously or not) in the Whitman tradition of rough integrity, he futilely imitates Pre-Raphaelitism, a prospect as likely to succeed as the assault against Jove by Capaneus. This unheroic Odysseus, too naïve to stop his ears, gives in to the lure of the sirens who for the first year detain him as he attempts being an apostle of ornamentation. Over in France the "thing rendered precisely," as in *Madame Bovary*, awaits his exchange of "magic" for reality. At thirty he comes to the sad awareness that his chance is over.

This insight accounts for the fact that the opening section is an epitaph. Mauberley's contemporaries have forgotten the stranger who disdained their commonplaces in his search for "an Attic grace." The anti-hero of the poem is ahead of his age in a desire to explore the mind, to make distinctions, that passion which inspired Cavalcanti. Unwilling to relinquish a hard-won artistry in words for "mendacities," he gives up his quixotic quest. Such a decision alone indicates that finally Pound has arrived at more than a "portrait of the artist as a young man." Though there is no reason to stress autobiography, the epitaph may belong to the demise of the young man whom the earlier poems presented.

Mauberley rebels not only against the current literary trend but against militarism: indeed, he is a modern equivalent of Propertius refusing to bow before "the grandeur that was Rome." Eliot in *The Waste Land* had expressed his own disillusion with the society which had drawn Mauberley across the ocean. Pound's *persona* sees it as an age too impatient for art, one based only on conformity, or what would now be called assembly-line products. Its idols are speed and mechanization. Mauberley is oppressed by its joylessness.

Through his stream of consciousness, confined within a sophisticated measure and rhyme borrowed from Théophile Gautier, he reveals his distaste for religion, politics, poetry, as he sees these three existing around him.

Against the sterility of these years in England stands World War I, terrible in its carnage, with young lives taken for nothing.

The rest of the sequence requires considerable learning, including topical information now buried in minor magazines and newspapers, if one is to appreciate it fully. That many consider the poem worth the toil needed for understanding is evident in that it is regularly taught in college classes and that one critic, John Espey, has written a complete book on it.

Three of its lyrics can be enjoyed in isolation. To this reader, however, the rest of "Hugh Selwyn Mauberley" is too puzzling and obscure to gain an audience for Pound. (Not all would agree with this estimate, for example, Norman Holmes Pearson of Yale University, who is very likely the most erudite of all explicators of the poem.) Such was not true in the year of its composition, when its figures from the London and Paris literary worlds were recognizable enough to illuminate it. Despite the thread of narrative, an overrefinement of detail leaves it for many readers merely a handful of clever fragments, without any Tiresias to give them coherence. Unlike *The Waste Land*, which has survived its source-hunters, the appeal of "Mauberley," over and above the sound structure, rests largely on the challenge of unraveling allusions, on social history, and on an occasional vivid phrase. Perhaps the main use of "Hugh Selwyn Mauberley" in Pound's career is the opportunity it gave him to try his hand at poetic biography, and in some passages at ironic self-portraiture. In a very special sense, it was a rehearsal for his masterpiece, which, in a qualified way, can be viewed as autobiography. Impersonal as much of *The Cantos* sounds, the poem contains whatever has been truly important in the life-space of Ezra Loomis Pound.

CHAPTER 4

Pound's Book of Changes

Some of Pound's best poetry is to be found in his translations, as exemplified at the start of *The Cantos* by his putting into magnificently economical English a Renaissance Latin version of the eleventh book of Homer's *Odyssey*. His theory of "the immortal concept," traveling down the years to emerge in era after era expressed by means of different media, has direct relevance to this aspect of his genius. Though his central thrust is to capture the spirit of each original, the vision informing the unique artifact and linking it with vanished splendor, he is no blunderer among masterpieces. Pound is a far better scholar both by education and by experience than philologists in general have recognized.

After extensive preparation in many languages, both in American classrooms and in their adjoining haunts of study, he traveled through Europe on a University of Pennsylvania fellowship, a coveted award, for the express purpose of deepening his knowledge of comparative tongues and the literatures written in them. With George Putnam's *Books and Their Makers during the Middle Ages* in hand, he investigated not only library holdings in the Provençal troubadours, in whose steps he literally followed, but also classics in Greek, Latin, and Spanish. Eventually, Chinese, Anglo-Saxon, and French joined the categories which he was to turn into English.

Most famous in his "Book of Changes" is the Canto condensation of the *Odyssey*, Book XI, the descent to the underworld. What Pound does here with the *Nekuia* is fairly typical of his procedure elsewhere. From what he has said in his criticism, one may assume that he would approve the following study of the first Canto in conjunction with the same section of the voyage toward Greece as told by another poet, Robert Fitzgerald, in his translation of the *Odyssey*.[1]

Fitzgerald, who has spent much of his life in New England, uses a sailor's opening: "We bore down on the ship at the sea's edge"—a yachtsman's account of men pushing a vessel into the water. Ezra Pound's "And then went down to the ship,/ Set keel to breakers" conveys, though less obviously, the same nautical idea, but it has the advantage of instantly striking the Anglo-Saxon mood, continued in "forth on the godly sea." Moreover, it emphasizes more strongly the epic convention *in medias res*. To landsmen, Fitzgerald's first word in line three is puzzling: "Stepping our mast and spar in the black ship"; yet his translation matches in effectiveness Pound's Old English "We set up mast and sail on that swart ship," the initial sibilants imitating to a degree the OE prototype. There is, however, a world of difference in power between Fitzgerald's "embarked the ram and ewe and went aboard/ in tears" and Pound's "Bore sheep aboard her, and our bodies also/ Heavy with weeping." Removed as far as possible from the music of the metronome, this second passage reflects a self-contained cadence indigenous to Canto prosody. Comparison point by point through the whole excerpt shows how E.P. saves words as he goes along, so that in his hands the section from Homer becomes a marvel of compression.

The older poet seldom relies on metaphor. Fitzgerald, on the contrary, imagines the breeze which fills the sails to be a hearty additional sailor "sent by the singing nymph with sun-bright hair." Such a phrase suggests the talent which marks his own original verse. Pound, without personifying the wind, merely mentions it, making no reference to Odysseus's recent hostess. Then he says: "Circe's this craft, the trim-coifed goddess," his phrase stronger than the lyric description above. As he goes on picturing the hero's journey to Avernus, he perfectly duplicates a fine arrangement of stresses in the second half of his eighth line: "Then sat we amidships, wind jamming the tiller"—//xx/x //xx/x. The four spondees "thus with stretched sail" achieve a more kinesthetic impression than Fitzgerald's "full sail spread," an expression devoid of onomatopoeia though possessed of grace and ease.

As Canto 1 proceeds, it keeps to the image itself rather than to a figure of speech. Thus Fitzgerald's "the flaming/ eye of Hêlios" differs considerably from Pound's simple "glitter of sun-rays" as both translators recount how mists kept light out of the Kimmerian lands, an unfounded belief of the ancients, from Homer onward, giving rise to the fact that the adjective *Kimmerian* is still used for gloomy; here at Hell's vestibule Pound's term creates an atmosphere not present in Fitzgerald's "Men of Winter."

Once within the infernal landscape, the Canto attains "an absolute rhythm" in "Poured we libations unto each the dead" as against Fitzgerald's "and poured/ libations round it [the votive pit] to the unnumbered dead." But nowhere in this Canto is the melodic genius of Pound more demonstrable than in "A sheep to Tiresias only, black and a bell-sheep," appearing in the other version thus: "as for Teiresias, I swore to sacrifice/ a black lamb, handsomest of all our flock."

The ritual necessary to permit the blind prophet's counsel proceeds. That knowledge of Latin which got Pound prematurely into the University of Pennsylvania animates the line "Dark blood flowed in the fosse," an idea which takes up three times as much space in Fitzgerald. Again, Anglo-Saxon serves as model: strength derived from juxtaposed stresses and internal rhyme characterizes Pound's "These many crowded about me; with shouting . . ." The other translation, though it lacks this particular asset, achieves an eerie, ghost-like effect in "From every side they came and sought the pit/ With rustling cries." *Rustling* before *cries* strikes one as just the right term, even though it does not fit the harsh, grim mood of the older rendering.

Possibly Canto 1 chooses Pluto to alliterate with Proserpine; Fitzgerald passes over the Greek pantheon in favor of the more general reference to the ruler, "sovereign Death." As the dictator of Imagism, Pound had preached, "Never an unnecessary word"; his insistence dominates here in "Till I should hear Tiresias" as opposed to "till I should know the presence of Teiresias." He omits the tears of Odysseus upon meeting Elpenor in Hades ("now when I saw him there I wept for pity/ and called out to him," in Fitzgerald's words),

merely saying, "And I cried in hurried speech." Prefacing Elpenor's answer by "And he in heavy speech," Pound narrates
in five words ("Ill fate and abundant wine") what in the other
takes twenty-five. The juxtaposed beats of "Ill fate" are one
more indication that we are in the icy world of "The Seafarer" and other lyrics of the Anglo-Saxon scop which were to
prove one of the sources for Hopkins's sprung rhythm. Con-
sistent with its avoidance of metaphor, the Canto keeps to the
place name *Avernus* instead of Fitzgerald's figurative "well of
dark."

In recent literary criticism the epitaph which Canto 1 ac-
cords Elpenor has been applied to Ezra Pound himself, who
though still alive is "*A man of no fortune, and with a name to
come.*" The notion of a specific "legend," or inscription, for
Elpenor's burial-spot is missing in Fitzgerald, though he does
include the promise Odysseus makes to his dead companion
about carrying out the memorial services requested. Without
any apparent loss, Pound next reduces a whole section of Homeric verse to "And Anticlea came, whom I beat off, and
then Tiresias Theban,/ Holding his golden wand."

The apex of Book XI is the prophecy uttered after Tiresias
takes the draught. Here Pound speaks astrologically ("man of
ill star") whereas Fitzgerald uses a literal description ("O
man of woe"); Pound continues the astral imagery in "the
sunless dead" as opposed to the "cold dead" and in Pluto, the
planet most remote from the sun, a more specific appellation
than "sovereign Death." The apostrophe, "man of ill star,"
though when written far from the life style of its author, has
for today's reader a tragic double sense.

The message for which the hero has come so far takes over

fifty lines in Fitzgerald but in Pound is reduced to "'Odysseus/ 'Shalt return through spiteful Neptune, over dark seas,/ 'Lose all companions.'" The detailed instructions for progress toward Ithaca are not important to the *periplum*, which after all deals with a greater personage than any Greek warrior: it portrays contemporary man, with the major elements that have gone into his consciousness, and it focuses on a destination more distant and more blessed than a city on the ancient Mediterranean coast.

The last tag out of Homer comes after Pound's address to his long-deceased Latin co-translator, Andreas Divus, whose 1538 version of the *Odyssey* had excited him into initiating the whole series of Cantos. The passage is taken from the middle of Book XII, changing the narrative by rearranging the trip back to Circe so that it precedes the trial by irresistible music: "And he sailed, by Sirens and thence outward and away/ And unto Circe." Since for most readers both Divus and the Greek text are inaccessible, such a paralleling as this brief one with the Fitzgerald analogue is the closest a commentator on Pound can come to any sort of discussion on how he "makes new" his Homeric prelude to *The Cantos*.

The same freedom with which Book XI of the *Odyssey* has been handled distinguishes Pound's "Homage to Sextus Propertius," in which, as William Sievert remarks, he completely transforms the poetry.[2] This rival in popularity to Canto 1 among the translations was composed just a little before "Hugh Selwyn Mauberley," like it concentrating on the downfall of England: the Latin satirist had much the same views as Pound on the decadence of empires. To Iris Barry, Pound wrote in 1916 from London: "And if you CANT find any decent translation of Catullus and Propertius, I suppose I shall have to rig up something." [3] What a casual instigation, if indeed we do owe the "Homage" to Miss Barry! *Polite Essays*, published over twenty years after this letter to her, classifies Propertius among those who really invented something.[4] Daniel, Cavalcanti, Catullus, Ovid, and the anonymous author of "The Seafarer" also belong among the "inventors." Another one, of course, is Villon, who conceived the medieval dream as "the paradise of the human mind under enlightenment,"[5] a rather appropriate designation for the culmination of *The Cantos* in the crystal sphere.

When Pound saw the truncated magazine version of his "Propertius," from Rapallo he roundly berated *Poetry's* editor, Harriet Monroe.[6] Although it was published in full at last in 1919 in *Quia Pauper Amavi*, a title out of Ovid, the adaptation got cut again in 1959, when New Directions issued *Selected Poems of Ezra Pound*, despite the fact that its length is not prohibitive.[7] Using as his text the Lucianus Mueller edition, Pound chooses twelve Propertian poems. However obtuse the reaction of reviewers and classicists, who are still taking him to task for temerity, he knew he had scored a triumph. To Felix E. Schelling he wrote from Paris on July 8, 1922, for the purpose of qualifying the word *original* which that professor had applied to the "Homage":

And "original"??? when I can so snugly fit into the words of Propertius almost thirty pages with nothing that isn't S. P., or with no distortion of his phrases that isn't justifiable by some other phrase of his elsewhere? [8]

He compares the tone of the dozen lyrics to that of Jules Laforgue (celebrated in Canto 116), in expostulating to Schelling about Propertius's renunciation of magniloquence,[9] certainly an attitude binding together Pound, Laforgue, and Propertius. His self-confidence is justified by George Dekker: "Unlike Mauberley, Propertius does not invite endless explanations; once we have grasped its basic conventions it speaks for itself remarkably well."[10]

A comparison of some lines in the first Propertian elegy of Book IV with Pound's English version discloses his procedure throughout in a way that description alone cannot do:

Callimachi Manes et Coi sacra Philetae
Shades of Callimachus, Coan ghosts of Philetas,

In vestrum, quaeso, me sinite ire nemus,
It is in your grove I would walk,

Primus ego ingredior puro de fonte sacerdos
I who come first from the clear font

Itala per Graios orgia ferre choros.
Bringing the Grecian orgies into Italy
        and the dance into Italy.

Dicite, quo pariter carmen tenuistis in antro?
Who hath taught you so subtle a measure,
        in what hall have you heard it;

Quove pede ingressi? quamve bibistis aquam?
What foot beat out your time-bar?
        What water has mellowed your whistles?

A valeat, Phoebum quicumque moratur in armis!
Outweariers of Apollo will, as we know, continue their Martian
        generalities.

Exactur tenui pumice versus eat,
We have kept our erasers in order.

Quo me Fama levat terra sublimis, et a me
Nata coronatis Musa triumphat equis,
Et mecum in curru parvi vectantur Amores,

Scriptorumque meas turba secuta rotas
A new-fangled chariot follows the flower-hung horses;
A young Muse with young loves clustered about her ascends with
     me into the aether. . . .

Non datur ad Musas currere lata via.
And there is no high-road to the Muses.[11]

Keeping to a word-for-word rendition, for the most part,
Pound, like any conscientious scholar, indicates by dots when
he decides to omit. He is not as cavalier as his detractors (or
perhaps better, "misunderstanders") would have us believe.

His language is informal to the point of colloquialism. After
all, a conversational diction is important to his aim: as he
wrote to A. R. Orage, "My job was to bring a dead man to
life; to present a living figure." [12] Just as William Butler Yeats
loved the woods of Coole so much that he wanted to go back
to them after death, so Propertius chooses the sacred groves
celebrated by two third-century Greek elegists, Callimachus
and Philetas. By this compliment he implies the influence his
predecessors have had on him. The most pronounced variation in the lines given above is the way Pound lingers over
his hero's introduction of gaiety into Italy, slowing up the
lines through stresses, repetition, consonantal stops such as
hath for *has*. Disdaining the path of political glory signified
by the pun *generalities,* the speaker wants to be with those
who climb the narrow mountain trail to the Pierian spring
near the Gulf of Salonica, haunt of the nine Muses. The
dozen lines might well stand as an independent lyric, mature
in prosody, and doubly meaningful in content when considered as a gloss on Pound's philosophy of life.

Cynthia, the only love of Propertius except for one very

early exception, had her burial place right along the high-
way. The poet desires another fate for *his* bones, in a passage
which is one of several in Pound's work that might be said to
be directions for his funeral (cf. Canto 91). Propertius has received a letter at midnight telling him to come to Cynthia
without delay. He debates whether to go and entrust his life
to danger; he knows that he disobeyed once, when such a
summons came, and was banished from her affection for a
year. Moreover, no one would want to harm lovers, who can
walk in the midst of barbarians without peril. The moon
shows the path, and Cupid holds the torch in front of him.
Mad dogs avert their bite; Venus becomes a companion for
"those who are shut out" (*exclusis*).

Very literally Propertius's request, which immediately follows this introduction, reads:

May the gods bring about that she not
                    place my bones on crowded earth
Where the mob makes a path by its constant traffic.
After death the tombs of lovers are thus dishonored:
May out-of-the-way earth cover me with its shady leaves
                                   [*terra coma*, or hair of trees]
May I be surrounded and buried in mounds of unknown sand.
It is not pleasing to have a name in the middle of the road.

                                                (my own translation)

In J. P. Sullivan's book *Ezra Pound and Sextus Propertius: A
Study in Comparative Translation,* which includes minor
changes from texts other than the Mueller, the author gives
Pound's rendition of this passage from the elegy thus:

Gods' aid, let not my bones lie in a public location
With crowds too assiduous in their crossing of it;

For thus are the tombs of lovers most desecrated.
May a woody and sequestered place cover me with its foliage
Or may I inter beneath the hummock of some as yet uncatalogued
    sand;
At any rate I shall not have my epitaph in a high road.[13]

Again and again, Propertius wryly expects few posthumous
honors, a prospect he finds amusing. These lines taken from
him by Ezra Pound echo that disdain, echo in fact Keats's
"Here lies one whose name was writ in water." Yet Keats knew
and Pound does too that their place will be among the great
poets.

Pound suggested to Iris Barry, only one of the young persons for whom he served as mentor, that she memorize some
of Propertius, "for the sake of knowing what rhythm really
is." [14] The symmetry of cadences (downbeats and unaccented
syllables) in the individual Latin lines is outstanding, while
the combinations of line-patterns provide a variety instructive
to any aspirant in verse. Hardly less useful to a neophyte are
certain poetic ideas, such as "Flame burns, rain sinks into the
cracks/ And they all go to rack ruin beneath the thud of the
years" (the clods of centuries fall on the buildings that proud
man has erected as if on an open grave). Some of these passages reach the "memorable speech" of Arnold's touchstones;
"Stands genius a deathless adornment,/ a name not to be
worn out with the years"; or, "And I also will sing of war
when this matter of a girl is exhausted."

Aesthetically, the selections from Propertius chosen by
Pound for translation have their peaks, as in the plea to the
deities of Hell to spare his lovely Cynthia, with its realistic
ending:

Death has his tooth in the lot, Avernus lusts for the lot of them,
Beauty is not eternal, no man has perennial fortune,
Slow foot, or swift foot, death delays but for a season.

This last line Pound as an older craftsman would have im-
proved by omitting the preposition *for,* so as to have "death
delays but a season," much more successful metrically. Most
praiseworthy of all is the elegy beginning with "one tangle of
shadows" crossing the Acheron, death having made prince
and slave equal at last.

Had Propertius been a ruler, doubtless he would have
found his place among the thrones of *The Cantos.* In his own
sphere, Pound ranks him with Catullus, Horace, and Ovid as
"people who matter." [15] Commenting on the place of this
Latin social commentator, Sullivan reveals part of the reason
for the American poet's attraction to him: "Propertius does
not feel that he can sincerely and without mockery write the
sort of court poetry that so many Augustan poets wrote—and
yet he cannot ignore entirely the demands for it. The result is
parody." [16] "Hugh Selwyn Mauberley" a little later was an even
clearer attempt to evaluate the age with a Laforguian irony.

As Pound asserts in the *ABC of Reading,* Propertius undoubtedly was not in the least inferior to his Greek anteced-
ents in the genre of the elegy.[17] Yet what miracle is going to
deliver him intact to readers who speak only English? Pound
does not pretend to be such a miracle-worker: he is giving us
a new composition to be judged as poetry in its own right.
Like most thinkers ahead of their time, in the beginning he
was ridiculed. William Sievert depicts thus the early re-
sponses: "When the dunces read his 'Homage' in 1917 they
complained that Pound didn't know his Latin, thinking of

translation in the first, literal sense, along with Dryden's Dutch commentators." [18] They missed completely how the Latin classic had been entirely changed, transformed into a warning to Europe and America in the ominous period just prior to World War I.

If Pound's translations were put in chronological order, they would form a comprehensive account of international prose and poetry such as that accomplished by his friend Ford Madox Ford in *The March of Literature.* Coming between Pound's Augustan satire and twelfth-century Provençal song is his rendition of· Anglo-Saxon lyrics. In 1912 he issued "The Seafarer," prophetic of *The Cantos* seen as *periplum.* His text was *Bright's Anglo-Saxon Reader,* as familiar to specialists as *Poor Richard's Almanac* is to Americans at large and still in use in some of today's graduate schools. Charles W. Kennedy, in discussing the poem, makes it seem a microcosm of that larger response to human and divine life, *The Cantos:* "Ehrismann regards the *Seafarer* as an allegorical rendering of the transient joy and pain of earth in sea imagery, with this presentiment set in contrast to the everlasting bliss of a heavenly kingdom." [19]

As with Fitzgerald and Canto 1, it may be useful to place side by side Pound's translation and that of another. R. K. Gordon's rendering of *Maeg ic be me sylfum soð gièd wrecan"* is "I can utter a true song of myself, tell of my travels"; [20] Pound opens with more vigor: "May I, for my own self song's truth reckon." [21] Juxtaposing Pound's verses with Kennedy's in *An Anthology of Old English Poetry* [22] will demonstrate the former's manner of making new. The lines are arranged in couplet form for ease of conparison, though occasionally an oblique glance is necessary to bring out the correspondences.

> Journey's jargon, how I in harsh days [Pound]
> *The strains of peril, the stress of toil* [Kennedy]
>
> Hardships endured oft.
> *Which oft I endured in anguish of spirit*
>
> Bitter breast-cares have I abided,
> *Through weary hours of aching woe.*
>
> Known on my keel many a care's hold,
> *My bark was swept by the breaking seas;*
>
> And dire sea-surge, and there I oft spent
> *Bitter the watch from the bow by night*
>
> Narrow nightwatch nigh the ship's head
> *As my ship drove on within sound of the rocks.*
>
> While she tossed close to cliffs. Coldly afflicted,
> *My feet were numb with the ripping cold.*
>
> My feet were by frost benumbed.

Pound adheres to the original much more than does Charles Kennedy: sometimes he alters only the word-order. He tries to make his alliteration match that in the text. Though perhaps he is less readable than Kennedy, his version has a ruggedness and a ring of truth which are impressive. The prose-reduction of Gordon shows by contrast how brilliantly Pound imitates the sea-surge:

how in toilsome days I often suffered a time of hardship, how I have borne bitter sorrow in my breast, made trial of many sorrowful abodes on ships; dread was the rolling of the waves. There the hard night-watch at the bow's prow was often my task, when it tosses by the cliffs. Afflicted with cold, my feet were fettered by frost, by chill bonds.[23]

Kennings abound throughout E.P.'s whole hundred lines: *ice-flakes, hail-scur, mead-drink, sea-fare, flood-ways, whale-path, earth-weal, sword-hate, life's-blast, flesh-cover* are quickly recognizable as vocabulary effects to be found in Canto 1's "changing" of the eleventh book of the *Odyssey*. The resemblance is inescapable. The same Anglo-Saxon diction and method of composing that breathes life into the realistic old sailor's account of his hard life on the ocean fits admirably the rigor and desolation of Hell. Not so readily discernible is the fact that the "seven-lakes Canto," 49, also derives from Old English poetics. Pound never lost that rhythmic conciseness which as a college student he discovered in "The Seafarer."

The thought, or better, theme, of the anonymous lyric was a foreshadowing of E.P.'s own later reflections:

> Days little durable,
> And all arrogance of earthen riches,
> There come now no kings nor Caesars
> Nor gold-giving lords like those gone.

The twentieth century has no Alexander distributing wealth to his troops; the flow of money is now in the opposite direction: from citizen to ruler.

What R. K. Gordon footnotes as obscure ("Though he will strew the grave with gold, bury his brother with various treasures beside dead kinsmen, that will not go with him"),[24] Pound converts simply as:

> And though he strew the grave with gold,
> His born brothers, their buried bodies
> Be an unlikely treasure hoard.

The actual meaning seems lost with the Old English scop. As do many other translators, Pound leaves out the entire conclusion of "The Seafarer," a homily closing, in Gordon's version: "Thanks be for ever to the Holy One because He, the Prince of glory, the Lord everlasting, has honoured us. Amen." [25] This omission may not be a critical judgment but simply a result of the circumstance that he was using Bright, who goes no further. However, as an advanced philologist, he very likely agreed with those who affirm that "The Seafarer" cannot be the work of a single poet, since the piety of the last half contrasts so radically with the Stoicism of the rest. Kennedy mentions this theory only to differ, though he does allow for a space of years between the two parts.[26] Pound's source, Bright, offers the opposite view in its commentary:

This poem is notable as an early expression of the Germanic enthusiasm for the sea, for storms and icy cold; even the thought that the landsman doesn't know what seafarers must endure whets the sailor's desire to set out on the whale-road. Here is a new temper in the literature of the world; no such enthusiasm for bitter physical experience can be found in classical writings. Unfortunately, after the middle of line 64 come many lines of tiresome religiosity which it is customary for editors to omit. It is to be hoped that they were added by a monkish scribe and do not represent the true mind of the original author.[27]

The untranslated part, actually gnomic poetry (which was often a collection of didactic commonplaces), fails to capture the valid religious meaning of the whole. "The Seafarer" conveys a spiritual significance akin to what a pilgrim feels on a cold rainy day at the stony shrine of Our Lady of Knock in County Wicklow, Ireland. The poem is a flat acknowledgment that this mortal life is one of hardship, to be faced with courage.

From the chilly, spray-flecked waters of the Atlantic to the sun-drenched fields and medieval fortress-towns of southern France was a "seven-league" stride calling for an entirely new way of singing. Provence was the country of Pound's dreams: the best thing about it was that unlike Camelot and Avalon it was real. At Hamilton College he had not only studied under but had become good friends with William Pierce Shepard, to whom Raymond T. Hill and Thomas G. Bergen dedicated their *Anthology of the Provençal Troubadours,* one of the finest collections in current university use. In the eightieth Canto Pound immortalized this exceptional professor ("with a head built like Bill Shepard's"), with whom he corresponded at least until 1938. As he begins to read twelfth-century French verse, he singles out Peire Cardinal in particular in letters to his mother written during 1905 from Clinton (YALC). Later the names of Raimon de Miraval, Gerant de Bornehl, and a score of others appear. Over a quarter of a century later, he writes Mrs. Homer Pound from Italy that he has had a delightful morning in the Milan library, the Ambrosiana, poring over an Arnaut Daniel manuscript containing musical notation.[28] Between these dates had come the walking tour of 1912, with Dante and Putnam as companions, a trip he describes in Canto 20. In 1937 he praises a Tuscan troubadour to his Japanese correspondent Katue Kitasono: "With Sordello the fusion of word, sound, movement is so simple one only understands it after having studied Provençal and half forgotten it, and come back to it twenty years later."[29] To his work on Sordello, the traveler through *Purga-*

torio as escort of Dante, Pound brought the knowledge result-
ing from his deeply rooted admiration of Browning's marvelous if over-difficult narration.

Halfway through his twenties, Pound put together his
insights and factual "finds" on the minstrelsy of Provence in
The Spirit of Romance, a third of which is devoted to that
subject. Those who are not interested in saturating themselves with *The Cantos* can obtain knowledge of his literary
powers, together with much pleasure, from this highly fascinating book, the mood of which is deducible from the Preface: "Art is a joyous thing. Its happiness antedates even
Whistler: apropos of which I would in all seriousness plead
for a greater levity, a more befitting levity, in our study of
the arts." [30]

In the same decade Pound had published a gathering of
lyrics by the Tuscan singer now of importance to the literary
world at large because Dante put his father in the circle of
burning tombs reserved for heretics; the son, Guido Cavalcanti, if forgotten by most readers of poetry, will forever
shine as a star not because of these sensitive translations but
because of the Canto which contains the meticulously refined
lyric of his beginning "A lady asks me." In the 1920 volume
called *Umbra,* preserving all of Pound's lyrics that he wished
to keep in print, and again in *Instigations,* one finds Arnaut
Daniel, Pound's favorite troubadour, well represented. In the
former, one might consider him the most illustrious ghost in
the "shaded area" or "land of shades" which the title hints at.
For Ezra Pound as for Dante Alighieri, Daniel was king of
medieval lyricists. *The Translations of Ezra Pound* includes
improvements on the "dry runs" of Daniel and other trouba-

dours which he attempted, inspired by his vagabonding through the landscapes which had changed so little since their jongleurs set to instrument their mastery of *alba* and *planh, pastorelle* and *sirvente.* Never far from Pound in his investigation of Provençal song was the indispensable *De Vulgari Eloquentia.*

"La Fraisne," "Cino," and "Na Audiart" in *A Lume Spento* can now be seen as preparation for the scholarly task of faithfully transcribing instead of imitating the troubadours. These three show a romanticism undisciplined by Pound's more mature "visions and revisions," which in the case of the Cavalcanti poem mentioned above never knew a period. T. S. Eliot has called "Sestina: Altaforte" the best example of that form in English. Besides Bertran de Born and the others already mentioned, Ventadorn (spellings vary), Vidal, William of Poictiers make their way from the lyrics into *The Cantos,* a narrative the texture of which is broken into by voices, often singing voices, out of history. Perhaps "Near Perigord" best gives the atmosphere of the region which for Pound had such charm that after his marriage he and his bride made Toulouse their home for a short while. At one time (between 1917 and 1918) he even intended a complete book on the troubadours.[31] That his interest steadily grew is manifest by the addition of "Psychology and the Troubadours" to the second edition of *The Spirit of Romance.*

Ezra Pound felt not only a passionate curiosity about the poetry of southern France as it existed in the twelfth and thirteenth centuries, but also a duty to promote translations of it, partly because of the salutary effect such an exercise had on young writers. In the fifth chapter of the *ABC of Reading* he insists: "I see every reason for studying Provençal verse (a little of it, say thirty or fifty poems) from Guillaume de Poictiers, Bertran de Born and Sordello." [32] So stiff-going is Provençal translation (the language is completely different from modern French) that even an eager disciple armed with university courses in the subject might think that Pound in this passage was joking as to quantity, but he is very much in earnest. Some of his junior contemporaries have gone to considerable trouble to act upon their master's counsel. I remember with gratitude the year at the University of Wisconsin in Madison when Paul Blackburn, then an undergraduate, recruited a small number of interested students, including myself, to take Provençal from Professor Karl Bottke. Many of our class assignments, refined, appeared in 1953 in Blackburn's *Proensa*, a revelation of the beauty to be found in troubadour song "made new" and a tribute to the influence of Pound.

So important did Pound consider Daniel, Ventadorn, Vidal, and their ambience that he entitled the first book of his to be printed in the United States *Provença: Poems Selected from Personae, Exultations, and Canzoniere of Ezra Pound* (1910). He was far less sanguine than was necessary when he wrote to Felix Schelling from Paris in July of 1922 that not only had he failed to convey the worth of troubadour poetry but that only a handful had picked up any interest in Provence from him.[33] Eliot has dramatized Pound's affinity to Cavalcanti, the Italian counterpart to Arnaut Daniel, by the famous dedication in *The Waste Land*. Indeed, the Whitman sentence "Whoever touches me touches a man" might be paraphrased in Pound's regard as "Whoever touches me touches a Provençal poet." In the best of his lyrics one detects the same thirst for precise distinctions, the same melodic inventiveness, the same psychological subtlety that inform the chansons.

From Provence to China, eastward or westward, is not so far as might appear when first they are coupled: critics of both painting and literature have pointed out resemblances between Oriental art and that of the troubadours. Botticelli, consistently admired by Pound, is a useful figure in relating the linear miracles common to both hemispheres.[34]

This poet came to see Chinese translation as even more challenging than Homeric, perhaps because through it swam into his youthful ken an almost totally unfamiliar civilization:

Looking eastward even my own scant knowledge of ideogram has been enough to teach me that a few hours' work on it is more enlivening, goes further to jog a man out of fixations than a month's work on a great greek author.[35]

In *Cathay* (1915) Pound published some of his best work, the translations from the eighth-century Rihaku (Li Po)—a fine starting-place for the teacher who wishes to acquaint students with E.P.—and lesser known Chinese poets. Sometimes one is almost tempted to divide Pound's career into before and after his contact with ideograms.

Having been entrusted with the Ernest Fenollosa notebooks by that scholar's widow, he developed an ever-growing preoccupation with the calligraphy, painting, verse, and ethics of Chinese culture. One can guess his pride in this gift of the lifework of the professor of Japanese from a letter to William Carlos Williams written on December 19, 1913: "I am very placid and happy and busy. Dorothy is learning Chinese. I've all old Fenollosa's treasures in ms." [36]

"The River-Merchant's Wife" is perhaps the most-anthologized piece in *Cathay:* a charming interior monologue by a teen-age "war-bride" who is longingly expecting her husband, "My Lord You." Daniel Hoffman, reviewing *Ezra Pound: A Close-up,* says: "The best thing in Reck's book is his printing, side by side, Fenollosa's prolix translation of a poem by Li Po and Pound's vivid condensation of its text into 'The River Merchant's Wife.' " [37] Another famous rendering from the Chinese is the twelfth-century "Song of the Bowmen of Shu," a ballad perhaps meant to be sung while marching or in a dance. In a desolate mood that recalls "The Seafarer," the bowmen, who left home in the sweet season of drooping willows, are sorrowfully returning in the snow. Still a third, Rihaku's "The River Song," overbrimming with paradisal imagery, glitters with "jeweled flutes," "pipes of gold," the new green grasses of the island Yee-shu, the blue-tipped willow cords tangled in mist "against the brocade-like palace." These poems require consideration as original lyrics, so distant are they from their brushstroke medium, a union of picture and song.

Pasted in Mrs. Pound's copy of *Cathay,* now in the University of Texas library in Austin, is a review from London's *The Times* (May 6, 1915), which lauds her husband for imitating the ellipses of Chinese verse, analogous to the unfilled space in Chinese pictorial art. One feels all that is not said in "The Beautiful Toilet," taken from Mei Sheng, 140 B.C., where the bored, pale young wife reaches out her hand to push open the door. There is no need to say explicitly that she will leave her drunken husband for a rendezvous by the blue grasses of the river, or the willows in the enclosed garden. The title itself promises an assignation.

Because of his devotion to the person and teachings of Confucius, it was inevitable that sooner or later Pound would try his hand at rendering him into English. Encouraged by the loneliness of the days in the Pisa D.T.C., where a Chinese dictionary was one of the few books allowed him, he translated the second of the four Chinese Classics—the *Chung Yung*, or what he calls "The Unwobbling Pivot," named for the fifth direction of the compass as known in China. Though the genius of Confucius as contained in this treatise on the unchanging mid-point had come down to the present day through the sage's follower Mencius, the work had not penetrated Western thought in any appreciable way. Few sentences of it give a better idea of Pound's method of composition than his explanation of sincerity as an activity which defines words with precision, "as if carved with a knifeblade." In calligraphy this sincerity is depicted by a lance of sun hitting the exact spot.[38] From the virtue comes intelligence, or inborn talent, the basis of education. Pound's version of the *Confucian Analects* in 1950 foreshadows the anthology of apothegm and anecdote which quite probably will one day be culled from *The Cantos*. Though the work is done in prose, the *logopoeia* of isolated sentences belongs to poetic speech.

Chinese experts have increasingly acknowledged Pound's competence. For example, John C. Wang writes in the *Sewanee Review* that "after four decades of conscientious labor, he finally published the complete translation of the Chinese *Shih*

Ching, with the title *The Classic Anthology Defined by Confucius,* in 1954, and won full recognition as a translator of Chinese poetry." [39]

In the 1960s Pound glorified Confucius above the rest of men when he said to interviewer Donald Hall that he intended to devote the last of *The Cantos* to recording the "top flight of the mind," with Confucius on the very top.[40]

Besides literature in Greek, Latin, French, Anglo-Saxon, Provençal, and Chinese, Ezra Pound translated, with criticism, several Japanese Noh plays: this material was issued both separately in 1916 and as part of his collected translations as introduced by Hugh Kenner in the 1953 New Directions volume. Pound's friend A. R. Orage, the editor of *The New Age,* disapproved of these: "The plays have atmosphere, and many of the speeches are charming, but head or tail of the whole I cannot make." [41] From the ineptitude of his own sentence his view need not be too seriously considered. While Pound's Noh re-creations are not as good as Yeats's, they are striking in their lyricism, even if the dialogue is more Celtic than Oriental.

In modern French his most extensive work is with the prose of Remy de Gourmont, who shared his Flaubertian intensity about finding *le mot juste* and was also desirous of depicting the finest discriminations possible, probably believing, with E.P., that "all education consists in making distinctions." The two would very likely have been not only correspondents but also personal friends had not de Gourmont died in 1915. He represents the intaglio quality of Pound's best verse. While a more extensive treatment of the French translations would be instructive, space requires a reliance on Frost's say-

ing: "All an artist needs is samples." Most of Pound's choices
sprang from real enthusiasm, but occasionally he undertook
translations such as Estaunié's novel *The Call of the Road*,
not because he felt any particular sympathy with the manuscript (in this case, quite the contrary) but because he needed
the money to support his family, including his aged parents.

Miscellaneous translations taken from a score of languages
are scattered throughout Pound's achievements. The most recent major one is that of Sophocles' *Women of Trachis*, unless
we count his collaboration with Noel Stock in *Love Poems of
Ancient Egypt*. His own part of the latter resulted from talks
at Brunnenburg with his son-in-law, Baron Boris de Rachewiltz, who had already made a literal version of these Asiatic
"conversations in courtship." *Women of Trachis*, probably the
most enigmatic of Sophoclean plays, centers on Hercules and
his triumphant realization that death is "the mother of
beauty," the finality of peace forming the thirteenth and
greatest of all his successful labors. The world may well regret
that Pound did not choose to do the first of the Theban cycle,
as Yeats had. While turning the Greek text into great original
poetry (Yeats worked from Jebb), he would also have furnished actable speech for the players.

Inevitably, an even more fervent wish will come into the
mind of many readers: if only Pound, while in his vigor, had
translated *The Divine Comedy!* He gave unsparingly of his
time, knowledge, and zest to Laurence Binyon when so engaged, just as he urged on W. H. D. Rouse in respect to
Homer. *Polite Essays* shows that none ever surpasses Dante
in his esteem:

One might indefinitely continue the praise of Dante's excellence of technique and his splendours of detail; but beneath these individual and separate delights is the great subsurge of his truth and his sincerity: his work is of that sort of art which is a key to the understanding of nature, of the beauty of the world and of the spirit.[42]

Had he been permitted a copy of Dante at Pisa, perhaps we might now possess at least a wreath of Dantean cantos as a chapter in his "Book of Changes." Instead, we have only the illustrative excerpts in *The Spirit of Romance* and the fragments scattered throughout Pound's own *Commedia*.

CHAPTER 5

The Cantos: From Erebus to Pisa

"An epic in the real sense is the speech of a nation thru the mouth of one man," Pound wrote his mother from London in 1909.[1] That nation, in *The Cantos* as in Dante, is the human race. The first book-length issue of *The Cantos* consisted of sixteen brought out by the Three Mountains Press of Paris, with fourteen more being added in two years to complete the 1930 *A Draft of XXX Cantos*. The main thrust of his effort in these years was to get down the colors on the palette. It is surprising how little Pound has altered the poem since his wholesale revisions of the first three Cantos as these appeared in the summer numbers of *Poetry* in 1917. While meticulous craftsmanship partially accounts for this lack of change, also involved is a desire to keep intact the record of his state of consciousness at the various times of writing. Even some of the discarded passages in the versions of the original three have been incorporated into the later text. The parts not used were perhaps the portrait of too young an artist; their images lack the stratification of *Quattrocento* painting by belonging more to the permanent world than to the recurrent and casual ones.[2]

Pound's serious interest in epic form dates at least from his undergraduate days. One excellent way to understand any author is to become familiar with the books he has read with care and enjoyment. In 1966 Karl Shapiro gave six lectures at Carleton College in Northfield, Minnesota, the first of which was called "From Aristotle to Dante." To the astonishment of most in his audience, what he really talked about was his bookshelves, covering authors between A and D. In doing this, Shapiro was actually speaking about himself. Analogously, an examination of Pound's reading serves to reveal his tastes and the sources of some of his material as if by intellectual X-ray.

As early as 1904 Ezra Pound possessed his own copy of Spenser's *Faerie Queene*. Always a collector, even as a boy, he also owned a 1713 edition of Milton's *Paradise Regained: A Poem in Four Books,* unusual in that it was illustrated. Those who consider Shakespeare's cycle of English history plays from King John through Henry the Eighth an epic would number Pound's 1864 *The Works of William Shakespeare* as edited by Clark and Wright among the examples of the genre important to his youth. The epic most frequently likened to *The Cantos* is Dante's *The Divine Comedy,* often mentioned in letters from Hamilton back to his parents in Wyncote. Good friends as they were, Basil Bunting and Pound loaned or gave each other books, so that at present in the Brunnenburg castle Bunting's 1920 Italian edition with commentary by Raffaele Andreoli rests on the shelves, near two volumes of the Laurence Binyon translation. Binyon, as the letters in the Yale American Literature Collection reveal, relied heavily on Pound's detailed criticism as he prepared his now widely used edition, the best, Pound felt, for a beginner.

In more than one sense, Ezra Pound was "the son of Homer." As all readers of *The Cantos* know, its substructure is Homeric, with an Odysseus-figure as the hero, part fictional, part autobiographical. All literature stemming from the Greek-Trojan conflict excited Pound's curiosity. By 1913 his books included Maurice Hewlett's *Helen Redeemed and Other Poems.* He also owned a much more obscure account of the fall of Troy, *The Epigoniad: A Poem in Nine Books,* by William Wilkie, which has an interesting introduction in defense of myth. One of his pleasures was discovering rare editions of Homer in bookstalls, for instance, *Les XXIIII Livres de L'Iliade D'Homère, Prince of Poètes Grecs,* its end-papers containing lists of pages and English words, written down in Pound's usual neat way of marking important points as he read. Also held in trust for him in the Tyrol castle are *Homeri Opera Omnia,* 1814; *Odysseae Homeri Libri XXIIII,* 1541; and the editions of the *Iliad* and the *Odyssey* in the Loeb Classical Library.

Under Pound's supervision, certain passages from his long poem were assembled in the fall of 1966 and published the next year as *Selected Cantos of Ezra Pound:* [3] those relevant to this chapter are from Cantos 1, 4, 9, 13, 14, 16. These represent the aged poet's advice to those who wish to acquaint themselves with his major achievement but feel at a loss as to how to start. Faced by its bulk, many hesitate, thinking the challenge too great. Others spend years reading without a plan. To have *il miglior fabbro* single out the best passages for initiation is therefore an enormous help. Entrances to the poem as recommended in Pound's 1966 book will be discussed in this chapter and the next.

The first Canto, the *Nekuia*, has already been taken up in treating the translations. Seldom does Pound attain the perfect union of music and sense with which the fourth Canto renders a burning Trojan palace: "The silver mirrors catch the bright stones and flare." The scene is also remarkable for its montage-like resemblance to an expressionistic film setting of a ballet: nymphs dancing at dawn in an orchard. This vision is paralleled, toward the end, by a wedding dance wherein "A scarlet flower is cast on the blanch-white stone," echoing the climax of the Provençal love-tragedy also found in Canto 4. The story is linked with Ovid's *Metamorphoses* by the introduction of the burden of the transformed nightingale's song. The French noblewoman corresponds to the father of the sacrificed child Itys, like Cabestanh a victim used to punish violation of marriage vows.

The second drama in this Canto continues the theme of Provence. Vidal, another troubadour, stumbles along through the forest, afflicted with lycanthropy, his counterpart in the Homeric world the metamorphosed Actaeon, who was cursed for looking upon Diana bathing, her "Ivory dipping in silver." This juxtaposition illustrates what Pound meant when under the pseudonym of William Atheling on *The New Age* staff he wrote: "Arts attract us because they are different from reality; yet differ in some way that is proportionate to reality." [4] The fourth Canto's myth and "fact," the latter varying from *vida* to *vida* in medieval manuscripts, reinforce each other repeatedly in an amazingly convincing manner.

The third key-excerpt as chosen by E.P., this time from the

ninth Canto, finds him deep in the history of the Italian era known as the *Risorgimento*. Besides Odysseus, the first major *persona* of the poem is Sigismundo Malatesta, sovereign of Rimini. Though Rimini and Ancona formed a duchy of only forty square miles between the Apennines and the Adriatic Sea, the area was a theater for the most passionate acts of war, revenge, and love. One gets the exciting sensation of being placed down by a time machine in the glorious age when the sculptor Agostino di Duccio was decorating the church ostensibly dedicated by Sigismundo to Saint Francis but actually a shrine to his mistress and later wife, Isotta. So fascinating were Tuscan tyrants like the Malatestas that Charles Yriarte in France and Adrian Stokes in England have written entire books about the *condottieri*, the first a leading source for the Rimini Cantos. Other background books owned by Pound are *Memorie Istoriche di Rimini e de' Suoi Signori*, a 1789 volume mostly about money; *Cavalerie della Città di Ferrara*, 1566, which he bought in Florence in 1923 while he was living in Rapallo; and *Raccolta di Lettere di Diversi Principi & altri Signori*, acquired in the springtime of 1924, a circumstance which helps to pinpoint his research into the Rimini saga.

Among the Malatesta dynasty, Sigismundo (or Sigismondo, as it is sometimes spelled) is the best known. John Addington Symonds finds him an archetypal person, like those in the second level of Cosimo Tura's mural at Ferrara, often held up as Pound's model for structure: "Sigismondo Pandolfo Malatesta, the Lord of Rimini, might be selected as a true type of the princes who united a romantic zeal for culture with the vices of barbarians." [5] Relying upon coins and medals, Symonds describes the man in such a way as to suggest Bertran de Born of "Sestina: Altaforte":

The whole face seems ready to flash with sudden violence, to merge its self-control in a spasm of fury. Sigismondo Pandolfo Malatesta killed three wives in succession, violated his daughter, and attempted the chastity of his son. So much of him belongs to the mere savage. He caused the magnificent church of S. Francesco at Rimini to be raised by Leo Alberti in a manner more worthy of a Pagan Pantheon than of a Christian temple.[6]

Sigismundo's zeal for architecture and sculpture relates him to Humanism. So does his translation of the body of the most famous of neo-Platonic Eastern philosophers, over whose ashes he ordered engraved an inscription which praises himself as much as the honored dead: "These remains of Gemistus of Byzantium, chief of the sages of his day, Sigismondo Pandolfo Malatesta, son of Pandolfo, commander in the war against the king of the Turks in the Morea, induced by the mighty love with which he burns for men of learning, brought hither and placed within this chest. 1466." [7]

Today the Malatesta temple at Rimini, known as the *Duomo*, is an excellent place in which to pray. Mass is regularly celebrated at Isotta's altar, as well as at the High Altar. The glory of Sigismundo's victories has gone up like smoke, together with his love for Isotta, to some degree built on egotism. But what he did for God, however ambivalently, lives on, and day by day enriches His Kingdom. Rimini's temple in the early morning is perfect in its quiet and devotion, the bareness of gray marble a relief after the gaudy baroque of much of Rome and Venice. A painting of Saint Francis shows the saint receiving the Stigmata, with Brother Leo at one

side; bright clouds opposite the seraph, descending toward
La Verna with the five marks of pain, highlight that messen-
ger sent to bestow upon the *Poverello* an identification with
Christ's suffering upon the Cross.

Only a few minutes away from the Cathedral of San Francesco is the Rimini *Libreria,* one floor of which is devoted to
art. Its book collection contains such relevant volumes as the
1794 *The Temple de Malatesta* by Fossati; Battaglini's *Memorie istoriche di Rimini de' suoi Signori,* published in Bologna in 1788; Ricci's *Il Tempio Malatestiano,* 1925; but, most
especially, Edward Hutton's standard work *Sigismondo,* London, 1906. Hutton's book enriches one's appreciation of *The
Cantos:* he says of Isotta, for instance; "Her hair, too, that was
the colour of old gold, seemed to take on the very aspect of
the day, and when the sun shone was like a veil behind
which someone was smiling." [8] A favorite concept of Pound,
crystallized in the term *diaphanous,* immediately springs to
mind.

A study of point of view from Canto to Canto in the Rimini
group discloses some in the first-person singular (though sus-
ceptible of several referents, like Whitman's "I" in *Leaves of
Grass*); others, in the third; still others wherein the narrator
seems an obscure actor in the drama. Passages illustrating
this last include: "And the Emperor came down and knighted
us"; "And we sent men to the silk wars"; or "And old Sforza
bitched us at Pèsaro." In 1444, Sigismundo's brother Galeazzo,
without any legal right, sold the city of Pèsaro to a rival nobleman, Alessandro Sforza, according to historian Symonds.[9]
This statement is colloquially expanded in the ninth Canto.

Travelers who visit the Ravenna mosaics and stop at the

nearby Abbey Church of Saint Apollinaire in Classe can still see its walls stripped bare of the marble which a hundred ox-carts took by night to beautify Malatesta's *Tempio*. Sigismundo was not one to worry about means and end. Whether the full four hundred ducats promised for the stone were paid, or only the two hundred listed on an extant receipt, is lost to history. The exploit was successfully brought off in order to accommodate Duccio and the other artists in the Malatesta employ as they worked toward the Greco-Roman monument rivaling the splendor of the *chiesa* Saint Apollinaire, mutilated by Rimini's ruler.

The last half of Canto 9 concerns a humiliation of the *Quattrocento* hero. It delineates the contents of his stolen mail-pouch—letters concerning building problems, Isotta's jealousy, the pleasure his young heir was taking in the father's gift of a pony. "That's what they found in the post-bag" of this soldier-king who furiously loved the enchanting woman, capable and dignified, whose emblem, the rose, appears everywhere in the "new" church, linked with his own, the elephant.

In the use of Pound's selection of spot-passages as guide-book, it is instructive to consider the titles he gives each. He labels Canto 9 "One year floods rose," establishing in this quartet of heavy beats the grave effect of retardation appropriate to an image of the advancing waters. Despite the turbulence which follows, this opening matches the tranquillity of Pound's fourth choice for beginners, Canto 13. Here, Confucius walks

> by the dynastic temple
> and into the cedar grove,
> and then out by the lower river,

conversing with his disciples Khieu Tchi, Tian the low-speaking, Tseu-lou, and Thseng-sie. Colorful as Malatesta's sway was, he is an ideal only in certain aspects, such as in his employment of Pisanello, Basinio, Duccio, and other artists. With Confucius, no reservations are needed. Acquainted with his writings even before emigration from the United States, Pound began reading him systematically during the winter months of 1914–15, while he and his wife were staying with Yeats at Coleman's Hatch in Sussex.[10]

Confucius praises individuality, condemns hypocrisy (as in the man who is elderly and foolish but pretends to wisdom), urges patronage of the arts, but above all enunciates the grounds on which Pound himself believes good government to rest:

> If a man have not order within him
> He cannot spread order about him;
> And if a man have not order within him
> His family will not act with due order;
>   And if the prince have not order within him
> He cannot put order into his dominions.

If Sigismundo was not able to achieve peace, the reason might have been that it did not dwell in his own heart. As early as Canto 9, then, one notes the idea underlying *Thrones*: a congeries of just men taken from many ages, centers of influence toward enlightened human behavior, no matter in what society they ruled. Some approach closer to others the ideal of "En la sua voluntade é nostre pace."

To leave Canto 13, with its Oriental pleasure spot fragrant with apricot blossoms drifting westward, and to enter the Hell of the next Canto would be almost too much of a shock without some sort of transition. Pound provides this by borrowing as a slender bridge between the two Dante's line "Io venni in luogo d'ogni luce muto," that lovely synesthetic effect of muted or silent light recalling Dante's wood where the sun is silent (*Inferno,* Canto I) and also the name of Pound's first book, *A Lume Spento.* At this point there occurs the second descent to infernal regions in the modern poem. One should resist the temptation to equate this interlude of horrors with those of the thirty-three Cantos wherein Dante and Virgil work their way down the ever-narrowing spiral until they reach the King of the Damned, Lucifer. Pound does not depend on a single line of narrative such as controls the pilgrimage of the Florentine and Virgil through earth's bowels, then up the luminous slopes of Purgatory. His symbolic journey does not, like Dante's, progress consecutively, as when, minus the Mantuan poet, the speaker rises upward to the very heart of the Divine Rose. Hell, Purgatory, and Heaven are constantly mingled in *The Cantos,* even as they are in this our earthly life.

Pound's Inferno exists for politicians, financiers, profiteers, pressmen, greedy mothers, murderers, bigots, vice crusaders, liars, slum owners, usurers, monopolists, other kinds of sinners, caught in a stasis of the ugliest circumstances imaginable. Often their punishment is connected with the excretion of filth, as if from the body politic. The region is unrelieved by that beauty of simile which keeps each of Dante's circles from squalor. By their frank use of Anglo-Saxon diction, as it is usually referred to, contemporary letters have rendered obsolete the omissions here in the text indicated by dashes; proper names, however, justice and charity would still proscribe. "The hell cantos are specifically LONDON, the state of

English mind in 1919 and 1920," declares Pound in a 1932 letter from Rapallo to John Drummond.[11] Like "Propertius," this bloc of writing has as target the all but complete miasma which Pound at the time felt England to be, infested by many of the vices personified, which here remain universal scourges.

Dante did not scruple to put his contemporaries, both deceased and in a few cases still living, within the circles of his *Inferno*. Pound, though elsewhere in *The Cantos* he uses names, thinly disguised, sees no need for identification: "Hell is not amusing. Not a joke. And when you get further along you find individuals, not abstracts. Even the XIV/XV has individuals in it, but NOT worth recording as such. In fact Bill Bird rather entertained that I had forgotten which rotters were there." [12]

Pound does not wish to leave the person who is reading *A Draft of XXX Cantos* for the first time wallowing in the feces of his contempt. Therefore, he recommends that an immediate progression be made to Canto 16. In this second Hell Canto, the "we" who have traversed this stinking realm of iniquity emerge inch by inch, as if given foothold by the petrification caused by Medusa's face glaring from the shield of Perseus:

And I bathed myself with the acid to free myself
    of the hell ticks,
Scales, fallen louse eggs.
    Palux Laerna,
the lake of bodies, aqua morta,
of limbs fluid, and mingled, like fish heaped in a bin,
and here an arm upward, clutching a fragment of marble . . .

The scene inevitably recalls Delacroix's remarkable painting to all familiar with this artistic vision of the crossing of the Styx by Virgil and Dante. Already the fertility of Pound's invention is steering the treatment of sin toward more attractive details than loathsome insects and various sorts of corruption: for example, the container of flopping fish, and the piece of marble clung to as precious by the lost soul. Looking around, the narrator finds himself in a paradisaical vestibule, an isolated beach. From here, like Aeneas ("and passing the tree of the bough"), he walks downward into an eternal dimension: that permanent light "as after a sun-set" where the founders of cities contemplate the splendor of eternal order.

The experience has been a vision within a vision, first of squalor, then of inexpressible peace. When it is over, like the traveler come back in the medieval dream-allegory "The Pearl," the *persona* discovers time and place to belong to the present. In Pound, this present takes the form of a spate of attacks, rendered mostly in a dialect or foreign languages. These range from country to country, bound together by the same theme, ugly war in its causes and results. The section is a remote preparation for that exhortation with which Canto 117 closes: "To be men not destroyers."

Somewhat corresponding in spirit to William Carlos Williams's *In the American Grain* is *Jefferson–Nuevo Mundo*, published by Faber and Faber in 1933 in London and as *Eleven New Cantos* by New Directions the following year in the United States. It presents in Cantos 31 to 41 an impressionistic history of the Cathay discovered by Columbus, picking up the development of the new continent during and after the days of the revolt of the colonies from England. Not only

does it prefigure *Thrones* but it continues the threefold structure common to *Quattrocento* art, wherein triptychs were
highly popular in church and *palazzo* decoration. Michael
Reck gives a good account of the conversation wherein
Pound confided to Yeats that this genre was one of his ways
of relating levels of being within *The Cantos:*

He showed the Irish poet a photograph of a fifteenth-century
mural by Cosimo Tura, in three compartments: above, the
Triumphs of Love and Chastity; in the middle, zodiacal signs; beneath, certain events of Cosimo Tura's day. Pound explained that
in *The Cantos* the *Triumphs* were replaced by archetypal persons,
the civilization builders (Confucius, Sigismundo Malatesta, Thomas
Jefferson), the zodiacal signs were replaced by *The Cantos'* fixed
elements (descent into hell, metamorphoses), and various modern
events took the place of the events in Tura's time.[13]

The "New Nation" group of Cantos chiefly develops the up-
permost level in the interpretation of the poem according to
Tura's triple division, Jefferson and the other founding fa-
thers serving as the archetypes.

Pound's reconstruction of the American past viewed as present begins with a Latin motto, "Tempus loquendi/ Tempus
tacendi," also chosen as headnote to the 1966–67 *Selected
Cantos.* These four words tie in episodes out of the struggles
of the young nation with the violence of the *Risorgimento:* in
the earlier century they served as the motto of Sigismundo
Malatesta. Together with the elephant and the rose, they are
observable in Rimini today, carved amidst the symbolic decorations of the *Tempio.* The meaning of the words was crucial
to the Pound who was engaged in this fourth decade of Cantos. In the thirties, the need for someone to speak out against

what was happening instead of maintaining a blameworthy silence seemed enormously important to the expatriate. He returned to the United States as a personal envoy to America's elected representatives and more concerned citizenry. Though he was convinced that the reality symbolized by the Liberty Bell so often seen in his boyhood was cracked indeed, he discovered that only in his poetry could he contribute to its restoration.

In the unpredictable way of origins, these Cantos are quite possibly owing to T. S. Eliot, who gave Pound ten volumes of *The Writings of Thomas Jefferson.*[14] Eliot, since 1927 a British subject, might have less reason than his friend for cherishing the words of Jefferson. Pound 'had resisted the desire of his wife shortly after their marriage that he give up his American citizenship; doubtless many of his European friends, too, had urged upon him this measure, which had he adopted it would have spared him the indictment for treason.

In the opening poem of the *Nuevo Mundo* series, Jefferson encourages Washington to urge that a canal be built across the colonized states to the "west country," a metaphorical way of representing what the entire epic aims to do, if *west* be taken as Paradise. Thomas Jefferson was a correspondent as prolific as E.P. himself. Elsewhere he writes to Thomas Paine, arranging his transportation from England to his home in Pennsylvania; to James Madison (partly in cypher) on the possibility of Madison's borrowing some money abroad to bolster the weak economy at home; to Washington again, ridiculing the incompetence of continental monarchs. Canto 31, picked out by Pound as most conducive to understanding the bloc, includes excerpts from several letters by John Adams to

Jefferson: in one such, the writer professes astonishment at how ignorant of government and history he has found Lafayette, Franklin, and other political leaders. The danger of these times runs underneath his words like the strains of a rapid, staccato music. From Monticello on April 16, 1811, Jefferson warns a certain Mr. Barlow as to the high importance and confidentiality of letters which Barlow will bear to Paris: "Most of them are/ of a complexion not proper for the eye of the police." The possibility of the loss of this mail is a flash-back to Sigismundo's stolen pouch in fifteenth-century Italy.

Typical of Pound's use of Eliot's gift of the Jefferson books is his borrowing of the amusing anecdote wherein Franklin tells what would happen were the rational creature man stripped of all his appetites, especially hunger. Pound's method can be appreciated if this passage from *The Cantos* is placed next to its source, Jefferson's letter from John Adams dated November 15, 1813.[15] This humorous relief is followed by two lines from an epistle written by Jefferson to a lesser-known contemporary, Charles Thompson.[16] Ten days later, Jefferson is sending a message to inform his countryman Mr. Carr that there will be a meeting of patriots for the purpose of devising a means of communication from state to state (again, this situation, like that of the canal, resembles the scheme of *The Cantos*).

Unquestionably, the 1924 two-volume work by W. E. Woodward, *George Washington: The Image and the Man*, from Pound's private collection furnished background information for his depiction of the age of the American Revolution and the period succeeding it. Another piece of concrete evidence of his continued interest in the subject is his copy of

Max Farrand's *The Framing of the Constitution of the United States,* a study published in 1958. He also owned Jefferson's 1825 *Notes on the State of Virginia,* marked by him "precious o.p." As was his habit, he annotated it by listing important page references on the end-papers. Still further vital sources for this section are *Jefferson and Hamilton* and *Jefferson in Power,* books by Claude Bowers which came out in the twenties and thirties.

Within *Eleven New Cantos* occurs the famous translation from Cavalcanti, "A lady asks me," patiently refined from the days of *The Spirit of Romance.* In the *Anschauung* of Ezra Pound, worlds as different as this of Tuscan song and Jefferson's *paideuma* coexist. The latter had its own diversions, but they were far from the intellectual excitement of Cavalcanti's sung definitions. One of the main functions of the "Donna mi prega" as inserted right at this point is to open a window on a horizon of infinite distances, the horizon of Dante's cosmos, so closely related in imaginative delicacy and lyricism to the verse of his intimate friend Guido Cavalcanti.

From the very start of his enthusiasm for troubadour song, this particular specimen of Cavalcanti, come upon in various bookstalls or little shops of Europe, had magnetized Pound. Wherever he went, he searched out rare editions of early Italian poems containing it, preferably with commentary. Among these were *Guido Cavalcanti Rime,* bought in 1931; Celso Cittadini's *Tre Canzone di Guido Cavalcanti,* Siena, 1949; [17] *Le Origini della Volgar Toscana Favella,* by the same author, with Egidio's exposition on Cavalcanti, issued in 1602; Gino Lega's *Il Canzoniere,* 1905; Pietro Ercole's *Guido Cavalcanti e le Sue Rime,* 1889; *Rime di Diversi Antichi Autori*

Toscani in Dodici Libri Raccolte, 1740, which has E.P.'s markings in the text of "Donna mi prega"; *La Sposition di Girolamo Frachetta sopra La Canzone di' Guido Cavalcanti Donna mi prega,* 1585, purchased in 1929. From his earliest attempt in 1910 right up to Canto 36, Pound labored perseveringly at adequately rendering this poet who so well incarnated in his own inquiring personality the temper of early Renaissance times.

Canto 38 is completely unlike the lively opening chapter of the *Jefferson–Nuevo Mundo* unit, rooted as this is in the heroic age of eastern America. Perhaps it is this complete variance, suggestive of the complexity of a consciousness extending backward to Homer and even further, which has caused Pound to select this Canto as the second of the "best ways" to enter the section of the poem in question. *Polite Essays* remarks: "As for the revolution of the *word.* It makes no difference whether we are writing of money or landscapes." [18] While his friend Eliot was finding poetry in river-litter, pimply clerks, strident Cockney voices in a closing bar, Pound took as his subject money, just as Dante had in the *Paradiso.* Indeed, the lines which preface this Canto come from *The Divine Comedy:* "il duol che sopre Senna/ Induce, faseggiando la moneta." [19] This excerpt out of the diaphanous widening crescendo of the Florentine epic is echoed halfway through in

> and the light became so bright and so blindin'
> in this layer of paradise
> that the mind of man was bewildered.

Most of the thirty-eighth Canto deals with the role that munitions manufacturers and speculators have played in "the in-

humanity of man to man" which is war. Then Pound returns
us to the world of that Greek who was never at a loss, Odysseus, in the middle of his Circean adventure. Falsification of
money, in whatever form this evil may rear its hideous head,
is equated with turning human beings into swine. The wise
leader of the Ithacan division of the Achaeans, fortified with
the God-given moly of intelligence, outwits the sorceress, putting her power to good use, just as right attitudes toward
money put to good use this necessary means of exchange.

To emphasize these thirteen Cantos (the *Jefferson–Nuevo
Mundo* ones) as a bloc, Pound ends them with "ad interim
1933," a device somewhat like the unfilled space, or "silence,"
of Chinese hand-scrolls. When he picks up the *periplum*
again, while singling out the passages for the 1966–67 anthology, he chooses from the section published thirty years earlier
as the *Fifth Decad* those which cluster around the Monte de
Paschi, Siena's remarkable bank founded in the seventeenth
century. The line "Thus BANK of the grassland was raised into
Seignory" from the forty-third Canto displays the conviction
that the root meaning of bank (*mound, fund, bottom*), a
meaning taken from Nature, ought to influence its operation
by keeping it close to the source of productivity. Over ten
times in this opening unit he refers to *Mount* or some form of
it ("a base, a fondo"), thus relating the bank to the favorable
connotations attributed to mountains by symbology.

Like most towns of medieval origin in Italy, Siena has had
a stormy history. Faction after faction controlled it, from the
Monte de' Nobili to the *Monte del Popolo,* until by 1620,
partly because of the intelligent planning of the two Tuscan
Leopolds, the reins of government lay in the hands of another

sort of *Monte,* comprised of those citizens responsible for the community's economy. The principles of Pietro Leopoldo, a prudent ruler who wanted state debts brought to an end, were carried on by his son Ferdinando III. Canto 44 eulogizes the services to Siena of these men by its joyous re-creation of an eighteenth-century celebration, complete with all the music, pomp, and ceremony that the Italian disposition loves:

Flags trumpets horns drums
and a placard
                    VIVA FERDINANDO
and were sounded all carillons
with bombs and with bonfires and was sung TE DEUM
in thanks to the Highest for this so
provident law
and were lights lit in the chapel of Alexander
        and the image of the Madonna unveiled
and sung litanies and then went to St Catherine's chapel
in S. Domenico and by the reliquary
of the Saint's head sang prayers and
went to the Company Fonte Giusta
also singing the litanies
and when was this thanksgiving ended the cortege
and the contrade with horns drums
trumpets and banners went to the
houses of the various ambulant vendors, then were the sticks of the
flags set in the stanchions on the Palace of the Seignors
and the gilded placard between them

All this happened within the space of a morning, bells continuing to ring without ceasing throughout the day. The morrow featured a procession, with bonfires in the piazza, bombs in great numbers, masquerade balls, and again litanies, end-

ing "Ferdinando EVVIVA/ Evviva Ferdinado [*sic*] il Terzo."
The description quoted above proves how right Pound was
when he wrote to translator W. H. D. Rouse during one of
his sojourns in Venice: "I have just done 4 cantos. Three
mostly about Monte di Paschi in language that I hope is natural. At any rate it flows." [20] His conversational rhythms in
the Siena sequence are as "right" as David Grene's translation
of Sophocles, or, for that matter, as the more famous one of
Oedipus Rex by William Butler Yeats. Another virtue of the
lines is that they have the plentitude of detail to be found in
an Old Testament chronicle.

Moving on to another center of European history, Pound
credits even Napoleon Bonaparte, power-hungry as he was,
with moments of civic sapience in the form of agricultural
and financial improvements. His qualified praise—" 'Thank
god such men be but few'/ though they build up human
courage"—takes us back to the *Quattrocento*, and to Sigismundo's prowess on the Adriatic coast in the ventures that
radiated from his fortress at Rimini.

Most anthologies of American verse contain Canto 45, on
usury. The best way of commending it is to urge that it be
read. Here, Pound is at his finest, both in meter and in imagery. He keeps the entire Canto within the third, or lowest,
range of the Cosimo Tura mural, that of real events. Against
the negativism of this lyrical condemnation of *usura* rises an
affirmation of the excellence of eight fifteenth-century artists.
These are Pietro Lombardo, the Paduan who decorated the
marvelously designed Church of Maria Miracoli in Venice (a
building all but idolized by Pound for its perfection); Agostino di Duccio of Rimini fame; Piero della Francesca, who

painted at Arezzo, Florence, Rimini, as well as in his native city; Giovanni Bellini, so beautifully represented in the *Accademia* gallery not far from Pound's later quarters in Venice's San Gregorio area; Sandro Botticelli; Fra Angelico; Ambrogio Praedis; and the Dutch painter Hans Memling. The defeat by Geryon of Siena's scheme for public welfare sounds forth dully in "Corpses are set to banquet/ at behest of usura."

If this were a thorough explication of *The Cantos*—Pound's lifetime in poetic mode, begun before twenty and still unfolding—what happiness it would be to linger at that "form cut in the air" which is Canto 47! Canto 49, also selected by its author as vital in any approach to the whole, is likewise a gem. Usually known as the "seven-lakes Canto," it is based on a precious album of Chinese poems painted on silk and illustrated by landscapes. Once belonging to his parents, this book is kept today among Pound's treasures at Brunnenburg, carefully wrapped in tissue. Noel Stock has related how a schoolteacher from China, Miss Tseng, translated the calligraphy for Pound on the rooftop of the Rapallo dwelling; [21] from the notes of their time together over this artifact he constructed a truly Oriental lyric, one which looks backward to his Imagist days and ahead to future preoccupation with Chinese culture in *The Cantos*.

The last Canto of the *Fifth Decad* is largely a repetition, with slight variations, of the jeremiad on usury, concluding with the first ideogram to appear in *The Cantos*, the *ching ming* ("precise terms"), taken from the third verse of the Confucian *Analects*, XIII. After being introduced into the epic, this sign will return again and again, with each use making more clear the reasons for its inclusion. Such incremental technique as is represented by the *ching ming* is a significant factor in comprehending Pound. Perhaps it ought to be enough to suggest that the whole weight of Oriental wisdom as concentrated in Confucius is thereby drawn again and again into the poem. However, even readers who have survived Latin, Greek, French, Spanish, Italian, and Provençal sometimes balk at Chinese. They can be reassured by critic Babette Deutsch:

The pleasure to be derived from recognition of his [Pound's] models is not essential to enjoyment of these sharp characterizations. Whether he cocks an ear in the direction of Propertius or of Bertrans de Born, glances back at Gautier or at Li Po, his feeling for words, his unique gift of phrasing permits him to turn the matter of the poets to his own use.[22]

Nonliterary sources (the history of Italian banking) are metamorphosed with like skill into the very stuff of dreams, not dissimilar to Dr. Williams's *Paterson*, though Pound's "local" is wherever his imagination happens to be, whether in some definite time and space or in timelessness. Eternity enters this decade of *The Cantos* as the unspeakably beautiful fertility rite in honor of Adonis (Canto 47), prefaced by the prophetic

> Who even dead, yet hath his mind entire!
> This sound came in the dark
> First must thou go the road
>   to hell
> And to the bower of Ceres' daughter Proserpine,
> Through overhanging dark, to see Tiresias,
> Eyeless that was, a shade, that is in hell
> So full of knowing that the beefy men know less than he,

> Ere thou come to thy road's end
> > Knowledge the shade of a shade,
> Yet must thou sail after knowledge
> Knowing less than drugged beasts.

The principle of fruitfulness, of bounty from the soil (Ceres) on which economics rests, finds its place even in hell in Pound's tribute to Demeter. Across these lines falls the foreboding shadow of that most harrowing experience of his career, when he himself took the road to Avernus, "Through overhanging dark," at Pisa and its American counterpart.

In 1940, when Pound published twenty new Cantos, he realized that their multilingual nature would cause consternation, with probably a highly unfavorable critical response. Therefore he supplied an *apologia* for his continued effort to make distinctions. It took the form of an explanation that not only English but also French transliterations of Chinese names would be the general practice: "Our European knowledge of China has come via latin and french [he himself had derived much of this from Pauthier's history] and at any rate the french vowels as printed here have some sort of uniform connotation." Then he outlined the section according to the leading topics which were to be taken up in each Canto.

The initial set traces the course of Chinese civilization from the Age of the Five Rulers to the eighteenth century after Christ. At this point, interest shifts to the career of John Adams, around whom ten Cantos cluster, just as Cantos 31 to 41 clustered around Jefferson. As an additional reassurance, Pound remarks that foreign words seldom include anything not stated elsewhere in English, though the translation may not always occur in contiguous passages.

In the *Fifth Decad,* especially Canto 52, Pound relies upon
the scholarship of the Jesuit missionary Couvreur for his own
rendering of the astrological *Li Ki,* or Book of Rites, one of
the Five Sacred Classics.[23] Originally only the first thirty
lines of Canto 52 appeared in Pound's choice of "main elements" excerpts, but his New Directions publisher, James
Laughlin, considered the Canto important enough to be reprinted in its entirety when he brought out *Selected Cantos
of Ezra Pound* in the fall of 1970. The part deemed essential
by Pound is a description of early summer—birds, sacrifices
to the sun, the white latex in flower. Again one is reminded of
the astrological parallel to the Cosimo Tura mural. The borrowed line "Strife is between light and darkness" has much to
say about the whole "plot" of *The Cantos.*

The appellation "Lord of the Fire" might well apply to
"Ra" Pound himself when his powers of creation are at their
peak. At the zenith of summer the "Lord of the Fire" is dominant. Laughlin's extension has developed the Eastern ritual
for almost eighty more lines than in the first version, bringing
it to the conclusion of the Canto; perhaps he believed the
whole requisite in order to stress how ceremony is vital to
civilized life, wherein men reverence the "Lords" of mountains and great rivers. The sun has progressed through the
signs of the zodiac, arriving at winter. The year comes round
full cycle, and it is spring again, spring when "Pheasant lift-
eth his voice to the Spirit of Mountains." Men and Nature
move in dignified accord.

Nowhere in his work is Pound's metrical vigor more evident. He loves to start a line with one, two, or even three
heavy beats ("No wood burned into charcoal"). To connect

the Chinese order with contemporary good leadership, he recalls what Yeats once told him about the Sligo of his boyhood summers on the west coast of Ireland—how Lord Palmerston acted as well as talked by draining the swamps around the city and by dredging its harbor.

Canto 53 is the second of the trio Pound regards as intelligent approaches to the "Chinese Cantos—John Adams" stretch of the poem. It contains the ideogram "make it new," an ideal inscribed in gold across all of Pound as well as on the bathtub of Tching the Emperor of the T'ang dynasty. After a summary of almost mythic rulers, Pound traces the royal families through the Hsia, Shang, and Chou, from 2205 B.C. to 255 B.C., down the annals of Chinese history. To indicate the relative youth of Western civilization, he mentions how, long before the Trojan-Greek struggle, the great Fou Hi was buried in a tomb which still can be visited, under "the high cypress between the strong walls." This circumstance serves the double purpose of dramatizing human continuity and of reminding the reader that Pound is not only purifying the dialect of, but just simply *telling*, "the tale of the tribe."

Make It New has become known as the title of his 1934 book of essays on world literature. Two years later, its author refers to this motto in a letter written on futurism to the editor of *The Listener:* "Marinetti's force and significance are demonstrated in his keeping hold of the root of the matter for a quarter of a century. The root is: MAKE IT NEW" (YALC).

Though expository rather than lyrical, Canto 57 is ranked along with Cantos 52 and 53 as crucial to an exploration of the epic as it resurrects the glories of China past. Like almost all of the *Fifth Decad,* it corresponds chronologically to the age of Sigismundo Malatesta; once again, as in the *Quattro-cento* sequence centered in Rimini, the narrator appears as a participant in the action ("we had a thousand such car-rochs"). Point of view when employed in this manner be-comes a device to heighten the effect that the Tiresian Pound has foresuffered all. In this China of fifty-three million inhabi-tants, learning flourished. Emperor Yang Lo ordered a *summa* ("that is that the gist of the books be corrected"). Cartographers created new maps. In 1497, "they made a law code." The ancestor of chemistry, alchemy, pursued its dream of changing baser metals into gold. A synonym for this proc-ess is the metamorphosis ideograph, the presence of which binds together this group by acting as a cousin of the "make it new" character.

One merit of this Canto is the way it provides a transition to Japan, subject of what immediately follows. Pound had al-ready perpetuated that country's dramatic art through reviv-ing, with Yeats, the Noh plays. Yet if one consults the table of contents preceding the twenty-fifth Canto, it becomes clear that the spotlight in Canto 57 falls upon the flight of Kien Ouen Ti in A.D. 1403. This uncrowned ruler is exemplary of exile: a youth conspired against, like Hamlet, by his uncle, he is wise enough to escape death by following some directions left in a box by his father, Hong Vou:

> Go out by the gate of Kouémen
> Under night dark, follow the aqueduct till you come to the temple
>   of Chin Lo-koan
> And in the red chest was habit of hochang and diploma of ho-
>   chang.

The fleeing Kien Ouen Ti and the nine mandarins who accompanied him put on the garments of monkhood found in
the chest: "and he was wandering for 35 years until YNG-
TSONG/ from one hiding place to another," never returning to
court. The theme of exile is nothing but a narrowing of that
of travel, which Homer, Dante, and Pound rely on to give
shape to their masterpieces.

To his Japanese friend Kitasono, E.P. wrote in 1940: "Sorry
Faber didn't print the MAP with my Cantos 52/71." [24] This
comment raises a problem of literary research fully as relevant to modern letters as the search for *The Waste Land*
manuscript, which ended in 1968 among the John Quinn materials on deposit at the New York Public Library. After so
many years when this text was believed lost, what we now
learn in examining the original version of the poem is not
really very much that is new about its writer, T. S. Eliot, but
rather the greatness through a specific illustration of Pound
as critic. It is unthinkable that any editor would have discarded this map. Neither is it likely, from the regret Pound
expresses to Kitasono, that the author should have thrown it
away. When and if this map comes to light, it will delineate
structural intentions not only in the *Fifth Decad* but in *The
Cantos* as a whole.

Right after the Chinese Cantos, Adams and those Americans of his milieu who constitute the American chapter of the
Sagetrieb return, not idealized, as in the schoolboy's imagination, but rather as very human. A pleasantry of antiquarian-
ism is the introduction of the older Thomas Adams, resident
of the Merry Mount immortalized by Bradford, Hawthorne,

and others. In Canto 70 his descendant writes to a friend that
the "aim of my life has been to be useful," [25] going on to say:

> how small in
> any nation the number who comprehend ANY
> system of constitution or administration
> and these few do not unite.

It is almost as if Pound had lived before, as if he himself were
putting to paper his awareness of public apathy. The quotation from Adams seems to make of Pound a *revenant,* a twentieth-century reincarnation of the statesman whose career embodied for him the finest virtues of the national period. The
true artist seeks always to reconcile the discordant elements
of his inner and outer worlds, or at least to report them faithfully. Before there can be the harmony of the "crystal sphere,"
heroic suffering must ensue. The Chinese/John Adams Cantos stand as the calm before Pisa.

CHAPTER 6

The Cantos: The Perilous Ascent

In his annotation to the Chinese–Adams bloc, Cantos 52 through 71, Pound remarks:

Note the final lines in greek, Canto 71, are from Hymn of Cleanthes, part of Adams' *paideuma* [culture]: Glorious, deathless of many names, Zeus aye ruling all things, founder of the inborn qualities of nature, by laws piloting all things.

These lines make a worthy prelude to the Pisan experience, wherein the protagonist of *The Cantos* required very strong faith indeed to see Divine Providence "piloting all things." The praises of God out of the classics bear the reader along with a steady, controlled energy, springing as they do from the sensibility of a man who in the seventieth Canto shouts in the face of the blackest adversity DUM SPIRO AMO.

On May 5, 1944, Pound was arrested. After some time in Genoa, ironically the traditionally assigned home of the Columbus whose daring opened up America to Caucasian civilization, he was transferred to the Disciplinary Training Center maintained by the United States at Pisa. There he was caged as no panther has ever been. His lawyer, Julien Cornell, through well-chosen images makes Pound's predicament live:

> It was now full summer, and the Italian sun beat down on the prison yard with unbearable intensity. A military highway ran nearby, and having no shelter he could not escape the ceaseless noise and dust. Although all the other prisoners were supplied with tents to keep out the heat and glare of the sun, Pound was given no such protection, probably so that guards could watch him at all times. Whereas other prisoners were let out of the cages for meals and exercise, Pound was always confined. While others were penned up in groups, he was alone in his cage.
>
> After enduring the tropical sun all day, neither sleep nor rest came with the night—electric lights glared into the poet's cage and burned into his bloodshot eyes. The cage was devoid of all furniture. Pound lay on the cement floor in his blankets, broiled by the sun and wet by the rain.[1]

Today the camp has been razed; outside Pisa, however, the largest military base in Italy is still in operation. To know exactly what Pound suffered in this environment is impossible, since from writer to writer details differ; one can safely assume that in general the circumstances as related by Cornell are accurate, since they must have been told him by his client. Even apart from such reports, Cantos 81 through 84 portray so effectively these months of incarceration that no one who reads them can remain ignorant of the great agony which Pound suffered.

Between the Chinese group and the Pisan section a lacuna exists, though *The Month at Goodspeed's* [2] asserts that 72 and 73 have been privately printed. It may be that discretion urges a temporary omission of these two because of topical allusions.

If nothing remained of the Cantos beyond those written during the days at Pisa, especially the twenty-five pages of magnificent poetry which constitute the seventy-fourth, Pound's status as a literary genius of the first rank would be secure. It is all but incredible to find a writer considered by some to be a major poet in English (Robert Graves) denying the excellence of these Cantos.[3] Their loveliness is the more remarkable in that they were composed in captivity, under most painful conditions, after a collapse from exposure and other hardships had necessitated Pound's removal from the 6′ x 6½′ "gorilla cage" of the camp wherein he was held in secrecy. These Cantos contain the basic elements introduced and developed in the first seventy, starred by certain "epiphanies" which act as preparation for the Edenic splendors ahead. Only rarely has Pound achieved passages of like beauty since that November in 1945 when he arrived in Washington, D.C., expecting to be tried for treason.

"What thou lovest well remains" (Canto 81). Even though his other possessions were confiscated, the people and places Pound cared most about could not be taken from him, since they were beyond the pale of military intrusion, safe *dove sta memoria*. With little occupation but the study of a Chinese edition of Confucius and the Book of the Creatures (Nature itself), he "existed" rather than lived, cut off from the vocal *Sagetrieb*, in that all conversation was denied him. As a compensation, he entertained a procession of friends, some called up from the dead, others summoned by the imagination from the world of freedom outside his cell. Instead of the hot, dusty vistas stretching from the camp's umbrella trees to the hills of Lucca rising against a remote, indifferent sky, he built immortal poetic "settings" out of books and places remembered from the other side of nightmare. For a long time, his whereabouts were unknown to his wife or his aged mother (Homer had died in 1942). The dreariness and anxiety of his situation overwhelming him, he cultivated by introspection former intellectual interests. Nowhere in *The Cantos* does he reveal more of his personal history, expressing in accents of humility his union with mankind's common pain. These "minor key" passages strike a new note in the music of the whole.

Pound's friends included the most distinguished artists of his age. Williams, Yeats, Hemingway, Lewis, Ford—these are only a few of the men linked to him in lasting mutual regard. An even more intimate bond existed between him and Eliot, whom he now recalls as he conducts his private *Recherche du Temps Perdu*. The same flippant humor appears which he had employed at Rapallo and Paris in successful attempts to shake free from melancholia his young London correspondent "the Possum," beset with family and financial worries. The Homeric theme "surfaces" as he thinks about W. H. D. Rouse, to whose translations of the Greek epics he had acted as midwife. Other characters in his mental drama include Frobenius, whose discoveries in Africa seemed to Pound landmarks in the progress of anthropology; Henry James, to whose prose he devoted more criticism than to that of any other novelist; Ernest Rhys, his associate in publishing ventures: "William" and "Fordie"; Upward, Bunting, Cummings, Vanderpyl, Cocteau, Beardsley, Plarr, Hewlett, Newbolt. Even those who were not actually dead were so to him, and Kensington as remote as Australia. "The Seafarer" supplies the rhythm and thought for the relevant line "Lordly men are to earth o'ergiven" (Canto 74). After resurrecting Pound's first meeting with "Jim" Joyce at Sirmione as the poet recalls it while at Pisa, Forrest Read says: "Joyce takes his place when Pound reassembles his companions of the 1910's. The city is a city of the dead, an Elysian version of Pound's London." [4]

The leading place-name in the heartbreaking lyrical interlude that is Canto 74 is Mount Taishan, which Pound knew only through his reading. In the Wyncote days, Asia had been a passion of his bookish mother, Isabel, who must often have shared with him the travel magazines to which she subscribed. Now all his time was spent in a "landscape" formed out of the image-residue from a past characterized by sensitive response to places. The distant peak (T'ai,[4] *great*) began to acquire a symbolic import similar to that assigned to mountains by Pound's choice among theologians, Richard of Saint Victor: "The power of comprehension of the rational spirit is like a big and lofty mountain." [5] In this part of *The Cantos* Pound sees, when the Italian sun sets, "the hill ablaze north of Taishan," just as, during the long Pisan nights, he pictures the constellations as being seen "from the tent under Taishan." His daughter, Mary, who was allowed to visit him for a half-hour in October, 1945, is "Περσεφόνεια [Persephone] under Taishan." Brought up away from her parents, the girl, like Persephone, combined springtime radiance with the sorrow symbolized in the abduction by Dis. To the poet at Pisa, she was princess of the *Nekuia*, or, as Forrest Read puts it, the city of the dead where he dwelt while under Italian arrest. The reference

> between NEKUIA, where are Alcmene and Tyro
> and the Charybdis of action
> to the solitude of Mt. Taishan

is interpreted thus by the critic Lawrence Dembo:

Nekuia is revelation; history and action are violence; Taishan is the final serenity beyond time, the psychological fulfillment of the poet who has mentioned vision despite his inability to make it present.[6]

The Canto's last reference to the Oriental peak witnesses to a peace born of contemplation: "How soft the wind under Taishan."

From vision to dream or dream to vision is a short step. The effect of the whole Canto is best caught in its initial line with the "enormous tragedy of the dream in the peasant's bent shoulders." Scholars seem afraid to connect this verse with the perhaps too "popular" "The Man with a Hoe" by Edwin Markham, though the Poundian silhouette is hard to separate from the social indictment beginning "Bowed with the weight of centuries, he stands . . ." J. A. Hatfield in *Dreams and Nightmares* says:

For these creatures of our dreams are ever breaking through the barriers of the unconscious mind to wake us up in terror. Or if wishing to escape from the monotony of the day we long for a haven of bliss, dreams provide us with visions of joy more ecstatic than those of the Arabian Nights, and allow us to partake of experiences such as we have never enjoyed nor are ever likely to enjoy —only to wake us to the realities of our daily life.[7]

Cold silence, barbed wire, steel spikes, heavy boot-tread, tasteless food, other spirit-crushing aspects of P.O.W. routine, and in no enemy camp but among his fellow Americans— such was the reality from which Pound was literally forced to flee if he were to maintain his balance. Not in sleep but in a reverie mastered by the discipline of art, the prisoner found materials for raising up "the city of Dioce whose terraces are the colour of stars" (the Ecbatan of Canto 4). Taking the fruit trees of the countryside as these bent under the wind, he united their grace to images from the China that he had revealed to the English-speaking world in *Cathay* and elsewhere:

> and olive tree blown white in the wind
> washed in the Kiang and Han
> what whiteness will you add to this whiteness,
> > what candor?

His thoughts traveled back to Gardasee, near Verona, that haunt of Catullus which Pound used to call Paradise when he wrote home during his twenties: "and the water was still on the West side/ flowing toward the Villa Catullo."

Pound's mosaic of past and present in *The Pisan Cantos* is unique in literature. In this poem, dedicated as was Dante's to love, he does not forget his cherished shrine at Terracina, with the breath-taking genesis of Aphrodite "from the sea Zephyr behind her." Diana, too, is marginally present when he introduces Nemi, home of her sacred grove but also of a lake known as the "Mirror of Venus." As he looks at his eucalyptus-bob talisman, taken from Rapallo as a souvenir of better times, he remembers

> To study with the white wings of time passing
> > is not that our delight
> to have friends come from far countries [*Analects*, I, 2]
> > is not that pleasure
> nor to care that we are untrumpeted?

Gone, alas, are his Riviera patio "and the wisteria and the tennis courts" where he was accustomed to playing five to seven sets daily. Yet even in Hell he can find Heaven. To Baudelaire's "Le Paradis n'est pas artificiel" he adds that often Paradise

> . . . exists only in fragments unexpected excellent sausage,
>   the smell of mint, for example,
>   Ladro the night cat;

These are details of trivial natural pleasures which assume gravely joyful significance in the gloomy microcosm of the D.T.C. Always fond of cats, Pound must have known real consolation at the welcome intrusion of Ladro into his night-loneliness. William Carlos Williams, among his friends, would best have understood this blessedness of "things."

During the all but unbearable confinement, Pound's senses, sharpened by his former studies of the ichthyologist Louis Agassiz, brought him relief from boredom as he directed attention toward the minutiae of his living quarters, at first the infamous cage, later a more humane but still crude makeshift shelter. So accurate are his observations as recorded in *The Cantos* that they seem the notes of a naturalist on a field trip: the squawky larks over the D.T.C. death cells behind the row of cages; a stepping bird with white markings; the almost chiseled precision of such a scene as

> and a white ox on the road toward Pisa
>   as if facing the tower,
> dark sheep in the drill field and on wet days were clouds
> in the mountain as if under the guard roosts.
>   A lizard upheld me
>   the wild birds wd not eat the white bread

He hears "two larks in contrappunto/ at sunset"; he sees a black animal, probably Ladro, the "night green of his pupil, as grape flesh and sea wave"; he notices how the dwarf morning glory twines round the grass blade; how the olive trees change from gleaming to dull as they turn in the breeze; how "the chrysalids mate in the air/color di luce/green splendour and as the sun thru pale fingers." Someone offers him "a new green katydid of a Sunday," its right wing torn off. How gently must his strong beautiful hands have held the insect, like himself broken by the world.

In this chapter of the *periplum*, Pound as Odysseus is "a man on whom the sun has gone down" (Canto 74). All of the subjects introduced as motifs in previous Cantos come back: the Rimini saga, "tempus tacendi, tempus loquendi" a grim reminder of the enforced silence; that wavering "shadow" of Sigismundo, Mussolini; Scotus Erigena and medieval optics as gathered together in the tensile-light ideogram, or "sun's cord"; China's emperors and Japan's plays ("and the nymph of the Hagoromo came to me/ as a corona of angels"); Wagadu, the four-times rebuilt city of Frobenius; Dante and the troubadours (Ventadour's "va il consire, el tempo rivolge" and Cavalcanti's "'fa di' clarita l'aer'"); fifteenth-century artists (Duccio, Pietro Romano, Pisanello, Cosimo Tura, Botticelli, Uccello, Bellini, the anonymous makers of sacred decorations in mosaic); Siena, where a face resembling his daughter's had looked down at him from the fresco over a Capoguardi doorway. While these console, they also demonstrate the truth of Francesca da Rimini's statement that there is no grief so great as happiness remembered in time of pain.

Now one of the living dead ("we who have passed over Lethe"—the ancient Greek River, not the Dantean), he remains alert to his infernal prison surroundings even while retreating to private paradises, the refuge of old men who dream dreams and see visions. In the background, mercifully, rose the alabaster towers of Pisa, their centuries-old aspiration lifting his heart toward all that his youth and maturity had most valued.

"Si tuit li dolh el plor," says Canto 84: truly, dolor rained down upon the aging writer in the Pisan concentration camp. Even while going through the dark night of the soul, he still can joke, relating with relish incidents of the past (anecdotes of United States senators, of his sturdy aunt riding a mule in Tangiers during their travels together when he was a boy) and not overlooking the few lighter aspects of his present environment (the soldier inappropriately named Slaughter). The blackness never becomes so dense that he doubts the existence of that brightness which he depicts through the brushstrokes for *Ming*[2], the total light-process, the sun in conjunction with the moon. Yet nowhere has understatement been more dramatically fitting than in the two lines that close this season of lonely anguish: "If the hoar frost grip thy tent/ Thou wilt give thanks when night is spent."

Indisputably, reading the pages of those critics who have searched into the facts at Pisa makes more vivid the predicament of the infirm American poet just before his transport to his nation's capital, a parody of Ithaca. Even without such information, however, the story begun in Canto 1 with the Odyssean descent into hell moves along its plot-line clearly enough from the text itself. A person does not go to hell once only. After his "homecoming" Pound was destined to explore even deeper chambers, particularly while surrounded by lunatics in Washington's Howard Hall, the prelude to Saint Elizabeth's.

Pound himself selected Cantos 81 and 84 as essential to understanding his whole work. Laughlin, his publisher, adds four and a half pages of Canto 83, perhaps because of its marked autobiographical nature, perhaps because no introduction to Pound is complete without the marvelous poetry that this section contains. Its mood is tranquil, contemplative: the meditations of philosophy (Gemistus and Scotus Erigena), the talk of writers (Yeats), the aesthetic experience as before the statue of Our Lady in Paris or the mermaids of the church in Venice. Beginning with "in the drenched tent there is quiet," we are with Pound at Pisa, where every natural thing reminds him of beauty known in the days of freedom—rain, hills, grass, clouds, sun, trees. Even in captivity, he can avoid emptiness of spirit, since he does not come under the category of those whose deeds are "not ensheaved and garnered in the heart."

Again, as in Canto 53, Pound seems to compare himself to Phoebus, Lord of the Fire: "the sun as a golden eye/ between dark cloud and the mountain." (To Wyncote he is still Ray [homonym of Ra, the Egyptian god of the sun].) In a state of suspension, awaiting removal to America, where the mountain, though it did not fall on him and crush him, remained to be climbed, he blessedly could take joy in the elemental things, reflecting, with his friend Hemingway, that "the sun also rises." Hinting from time to time at the prospect of a realm of crystalline permanence, the Pisan narrative restores the strength of its hero with a promise of a lasting oasis beyond the mountains and deserts ahead.

How unimportant, in the face of *The Pisan Cantos* as it stands today, seems all the resentment caused by the award-

ing of the Bollingen Prize to it as the outcome of the deliber-
ations of thirteen of America's most knowledgeable judges of
poetry, who stood by their decision that "out of all this
beauty something must come" (Canto 84). One is reminded of
the Lilliputians who swarmed over bound Gulliver, each (in
the case of Pound) armed with a poisoned spear. In the
words of the Pisan complex: "well those days are gone forever." The detraction has disappeared, and the poem remains
"like the best ancient greek coinage" or "a Madonna nove-
cento."

Pound takes the title for his sixth division, *Section: Rock-
Drill* (Cantos 85 to 95), from Sir Jacob Epstein's sculpture
which he was privileged to watch as it emerged into being in
the maker's studio. Now in London's Tate Gallery, this work,
remarkable in Pound's eyes for its elevation of pure form,
effectively provides a central metaphor on this level; moreover, it signifies his own constant effort to drive home the
ideas upon which the right kind of society rests. Executed at
first in plaster (1913), it was intended for automation, a plan
which Epstein later abandoned, casting only the top part in
gunmetal. In March of 1915, it formed part of the Vorticist
exhibition at the Doré Gallery, together with paintings by
Edward Wadsworth and Wyndham Lewis and sculpture by
Gaudier-Brzeska.[8] The relevance of its title to *Blast*, the
organ of Vorticism named by Pound himself, is pointed up by
Lewis's essay "The Rock Drill," a review of Pound's letters as
edited by Paige. The English painter attributes the concept
behind Epstein's work to his friend Pound: "You see him
hammering away, in letter after letter, at the reluctant Harriet Monroe, editor of the American magazine *Poetry*."[9]

Lewis had plenty of exposure to E.P.'s artistic code in those weekly meetings presided over by A. R. Orage of *The New Age* in London during the second decade of the century: these were seminars in the deepest sense of that word. "His rock-drill action," Lewis writes, "is impressive: he blasts away tirelessly, prodding and coaxing its mulish editors." [10]

In Pound's selection of passages from the epic which afford access into its multiplicity, he chooses three from *Section: Rock-Drill*—from the opening Canto, then from 93, and finally the entire closing Canto. All are illustrative of the strategies used throughout the poetry he composed while undergoing the trials of Saint Elizabeth's. The book leads off with the ideogram *Ling* [2], which stands for the sensibility of the Shang dynasty, a period of Chinese culture enduring five hundred and eighty years, almost down to the time of that civilization depicted in the *Odyssey*. As the Canto progresses, Pound presents in several different ways an ideal set up years earlier in his *Antheil and the Treatise on Harmony:* "The thorough artist is constantly trying to form the ideograph of 'the good' in his art; I mean the ideograph of admirable compound-of-qualities that make any work of art permanent." [11] The sun-moon *Ming* [2] character, the sign of the twenty-first dynasty, is perhaps the nearest synonym for such a combination of qualities among the samples of Chinese calligraphy that he incorporates into his poetic "portrait of a life." The "total light-process," it includes by implication the Four Tuan: love, benevolence or humanity, wisdom or knowledge, and propriety. Also belonging to artistic completeness are the connotations of the *hsein* [2] form, according to lexicographer Mathews applicable to the virtuous or worthy.[12] Related terms are rectitude (*li*³⁻⁴), to be used again in Canto 98; sincere (*ch'en* ²); and the ideogram showing a man looking into his own heart (*tê*), which is the Chinese way of depicting virtue, moral excellence, energy, power.

The Virgilian presence in the *Rock-Drill* journey through civilization is Tch'eng T'ang. This ruler, who lived over seventeen hundred years before Christ, is connected to our era in that peasant women both in his reign and in modern Italy enact a fertility ritual by concealing cocoons in their aprons at Easter: a continuity as impressive as the fusion of centuries, level by level, in Rome's Church of Saint Clement. T'ang's was an age of superlative awareness: repeatedly this noun appears. The condition of being so is described as restful, a state in which the five laws are rooted. Much of Canto 85 is a vernacular translation of the *Chou King* via the French Jesuit missionary Couvreur, key-source in Pound. A freely rendered passage of his commentary on these laws runs: "If you observe the five great rules of social relations sincerely each will reform himself and advance in the great way of perfection." [13] It would seem that anyone who can understand the formal prose of the French missionary can understand the livelier incorporations based on it as these appear in *Section: Rock-Drill*. While a comparison of the two will afford satisfaction to the scholar, it is not even as necessary as the juxtaposition of any English translation of the eleventh book of the *Odyssey* to Canto 1, which cannot help revealing to brilliant advantage the economy of Ezra Pound. This opinion is debatable: Donald Davie asserts, "Canto 85 has to be read along with its source; there is no other way to read it." [14] It seems to me, however, that Couvreur's material is merely a more dignified version than Pound's of excerpts from the *Chou King*, which are perfectly clear without reference to any translator.

One example of Pound's reliance on Couvreur can serve as the figure according to which he weaves his carpet: "The practice of true virtue reposes the heart and makes it better each day. A hypocritical conduct fatigues the heart and renders it each day more powerless," [15] which becomes in *The Cantos* "Awareness restful & fake is fatiguing." The fullness of such awareness returns as a souvenir of his sculptor-friend Brancusi's conversation, annotated by Pound in "Demarcations":

ONE OF THOSE DAYS WHEN I WOULD NOT HAVE GIVEN UP FIFTEEN MINUTES OF MY TIME FOR ANYTHING UNDER HEAVEN. There speaks the supreme sense of human values. There speaks WORK unbartered. That is the voice of humanity in its highest possible manifestation. [16]

Interested as always in sound government, Pound emphasizes in Canto 85 the preservation of records; to scatter them is to violate the *hsien* [2] form. He advocates standing for principle instead of thoughtlessly acting with the majority, which leads to what Canto 95 calls "the enormous organized cowardice." He praises straightforwardness rather than contriving; "know-how" added to a self-understanding born of contemplation; peace instead of argument; industry ("nor sitting down on a job that is done"); a just price; the sharing by subjects as well as rulers in the fruits of culture; freedom rather than oppression. Composed in eclectic fashion, his eulogy contains nothing really new to *The Cantos*, nor will its content be forgotten as he moves forward toward the "crystal sphere."

Roy Harvey Pearce, one of the critics who try to comprehend Pound instead of depreciating his achievement, writes enthusiastically about this span of the poem:

The Pisan Cantos stabilize the whole, in preparation for the series of almost mosaic pronouncements of the *Rock-Drill Cantos* (85–95). Here, as the working title indicates, Pound would drill holes for explosives, so as to move mountains and collect that part of them worth making new. These *Cantos* move with a rush of new insight; the ideogrammic mode achieves its fullest and richest and most literal use.[17]

For Pearce, the most striking explorer in the sequence is Apollonius of Tyana, whose story is told by Philostratus; Apollonius is a noted addition to the catalogue of *personae* assumed by Pound throughout the epic. Although the honoring of just rulers is not to be developed until *Thrones*, Y Yin of *Section: Rock-Drill*, minister under the first Shang emperor, might easily take his place among those elect to whom the next book of Cantos will be dedicated. Not only do the characters of Y Yin's name mean *earnest, sincere,* and in their verbal usage *to rule,* but Pound remarks that in Y Yin's day the seeds of high culture were already present. The emperor's prudent counselor is pictured as sending out the young king to contemplate so that he might more intelligently exercise his power. Again, manipulation of point of view brings about identification between the author and persons living in eras long before his: "Our dynasty came in because of a great sensibility." His several references to historic instances of good governing offer to him as to all citizens of his modern day a real opportunity to learn: "Our science is from the watching of shadows." Exempla of these shadows are Odysseus, Alexander, Cleopatra, Elizabeth I, Wellington, Hia (the monarch immediately preceding T'ang). Through oral tradition (*Sagetrieb*, or "the tale of the tribe") contemporary leaders can profit from the advice of the past to "respect the awareness and / train the fit men."

To pretend to grasp everything in Canto 85 would be misleading and pretentious; to attempt minute explication, even of that part clarified through patient study, would be out of place in an introduction such as this. The best initial approach might be to sum up the drift of the Canto by returning to a sentence in *The Spirit of Romance:* "It is an ancient hypothesis that the little cosmos 'corresponds' to the greater, that man has in him both sun and 'moon.' "[18] Thus no real contradiction ensues when the two are given as shining together, as in the *Ming*[2] ideogram with which this Canto closes, a symbol epitomizing the peak of human achievement.

When we move on to the remaining Cantos, we can do so with confidence that what we hear and see (in the case of the few untranscribed ideograms only see) will return illumined in various ways as the poem develops. Pound does not disappoint us in this hope. *Thrones* will have stamped on its cover the *Ling*[2] sign, showing a cloud, three mouths (or voices), two human forms. Mathews defines this sign as "the spirit of a being, which acts upon others," a meaning evident in "la vertu fleurit," which is placed next to it in that part of the Canto following the passage chosen for *Selected Cantos of Ezra Pound,* the guidebook for the novice and the intensely interesting (to the expert) assemblage of colors for the palette, together with hints as to what design these elements were meant to achieve. The *Ling* [2] sensibility is called "basis of rule," connecting it with one of the strongest themes in the book.

Noel Stock condenses Canto 86 thus:

Canto 86 is a brief history of Europe, or a collection of what Pound might call significant data on the history of Europe, from Talleyrand to Mussolini, with an occasional quick look at earlier periods as far back as Babylon.[19]

Sometimes one country, sometimes another gets prominence, but never do the primary virtues vary; all continue to stem from Confucius.

Canto 88 returns to the Jefferson-Adams complex in its eagerness to drive home Pound's monetary theories. Twenty years before the publication of *Section: Rock-Drill*, Pound described its method to his friend Basil Bunting: "The poet's job is to DEFINE and yet again define until the detail of surface is in accord with the root in justice." [20] Scenes as if out of a play with its subject the building of a new nation act as "detail" in this Canto. John Randolph is brought before us as he is about to engage in a duel with Henry Clay, his seconds Tatnall and Hamilton. This incident and others come from the pages of Thomas Hart Benton's nineteenth-century *Thirty Years' View*.

Government in Canto 88 is linked to the opening of the *Rock-Drill* series by its reference to Emperor T'ching of the exotic bathtub, who took copper from Chinese mines in accordance with the "distributive function of money." The rest of the Canto, punctuated by several digressions as to similar situations, features the exploitation of America by corporations unchecked by federal control and dominated by usury. The tone is remarkably calm on the whole in view of how emphatic Pound usually is in regard to the misuse of money. The four suits of a deck of cards (the spade inverted) at the end of Canto 88 indicate the Goddess Fortuna in a way not unrelated to Eliot in his employment of the Tarot pack.

Martin Van Buren was not exactly a mute and inglorious president, but neither is he a particularly celebrated one in the twentieth century. Canto 95 praises him indirectly. Probably its sentence with the strongest emotional appeal is that spoken by a person who holds "a hand without face cards," yet can say: "And there is something decent in the universe/ if I can feel all this": mist weighing down the wild thyme plants; the sounds in the oak wood; the exquisite paean to Leucothoe; the "light there almost solid"; his friend "Miss Ida by the bars in the jail house." The closest rival to this excellence in the Canto (some will think, its victor) is "and if I see her not/ No sight is worth the beauty of my thought."

The arrival at some lyrical passages in *The Cantos* is always a relief:

> LOVE, gone as lightning,
> > enduring 5000 years.
> Shall the comet cease moving
> > or the great stars be tied in one place!

Rapallo now comes back in the wild thyme reference, that fragrant herb which Pound elsewhere directs be placed over his grave. At this point of his career, the "immense cowardice of advertised litterati" (letters to the editors of the *Saturday*

Review and *Esquire* after the Bollingen award give some idea
of which authors he meant) seems quite likely to let him remain at Saint Elizabeth's until he dies. But he never gives up,
any more than Odysseus did. Leucothoe, who saved the
Greek hero on his way back to Ithaca, is once more introduced as a bringer of light, the white Leucothoe, "white
foam, a sea-gull." She promises him her scarf (bikini), better
for survival purposes than any raft: the help of God is might-
ier than human strategy. Even if he (Pound) is "drawn down
under the wave," he anticipates shipwreck bravely:

> That the wave crashed, whirling the raft, then
> Tearing the oar from his hand,
>   broke mast and yard-arm
> And he was drawn down under wave,
>   The wind tossing,
> Notus, Boreas,
>   as it were thistle-down.
> Then Leucothea had pity,
>   "mortal once
> Who now is a sea-god:

The Canto breaks off with the Homeric phrase ". . . thy way
to the land of the Phaeacians" in its original Greek text.[21]

Moving from one identity to another in *Section: Rock-Drill,*
Pound gives an impression of impersonality, but actually he
is transforming the events of his own life into art. At least one
critic, Clark Emery, finds a sharply autobiographical significance not only in the Pisan Cantos but also, to an even
greater degree, in the succeeding eleven:

As has been indicated, however, in the Pisan and *Rock-Drill* sections, the autobiographical and mythical levels are assimilated into

one to a degree not the case in the earlier cantos. In the Pisans, Pound undergoing the dark night of the soul, out of harmony with the process (as Odysseus was with the gods) but surviving against odds to learn humility and compassion, is to be seen constantly in close relation with his mythic images. And in the *Rock-Drill*, as he approaches that harmony, the relation is even closer.[22]

Unbroken as the arc of a sea-bird's flight, the joining of *Section: Rock-Drill* and *Thrones* is but another chapter in the Odyssean *fabula* which as in Joyce is coterminous with its author's masterwork. The protagonist is swallowed under by the wine-dark sea, then rises to catch, amidst the foamy billows, Leucothoe's garment, the incarnation of that divine assistance which alone will enable him to reach harbor. Drawing upon the words of Homer printed in Greek, Pound ends one volume and begins the next praising the goddess who has rescued him. No use of the epic convention *deus ex machina* is more persistent throughout the later Cantos.

Like progress in swimming, reading the next division, *Thrones*, is a gradual advance, and just as voluntary. No one tries to learn to swim by diving off a high springboard. If what we desire is an experience of the whole drama *Pound as Odysseus*, we cannot expect to feel at home by considering any one published volume separately. As the folk saying has it, "You can't get to Heaven in a rocking chair" (Dante's term is "feather bed"). Pound interrupts the first Canto of *Thrones* to remark on this factor of difficulty and also that of choice:

If we never write anything save what is already understood, the field of understanding will never be extended. One demands the right, now and again, to write for a few people with special interests and whose curiosity reaches into greater detail.

The Cantos in its entirety belongs to what he has called the work of "inventors," and while a first reading may yield gleams of loveliness and snatches of song, most of *Thrones* takes an apprenticeship. Its method continues to be that used in *The Waste Land* as it weaves fragments into a central metaphor, more difficult to recognize than Crane's bridge but not the chaos that some critics assert it to be, even as Tate and others affirmed chaos of Crane's monumental creation. Published soon after the dismissal of the indictment for treason (April 18, 1958), *Thrones* is a tapestry of histories with several passages which are as moving and original as comparable ones in the Pisan group. These interludes in the midst of a largely unlyrical section are outstanding for their individual flashes of imagery and for their lingering music.

In the seventh Canto of the *Inferno* Dante mentions certain angels as guides ruling the heavens so that their light as they revolve will be distributed equally (ll. 72–77). From one of this group of tutelary spirits Pound takes the title for *Thrones. Paradiso* pictures the Heaven of Saturn as being rotated by celestial spirits called Thrones,[23] though in *De Convivio* Dante had assigned these to the third sphere, that of Venus. In the interview with Donald Hall, Pound discusses his adaptation of Dante:

The thrones in Dante's *Paradiso* are for the spirits of the people who have been responsible for good government. The thrones in the Cantos are an attempt to move out from egoism and to establish some definition of an order possible or at least conceivable on earth. One is held up by the low percentage of reason which seems to operate in human affairs. *Thrones* concerns the states of mind of people responsible for something more than their personal conduct.[24]

The fourfold approach of Dante, moving from literal on the simplest level to anagogical, is at least implied here: (*a*) the actual figures, such as Justinian the Great; (*b*) realms of consciousness (an excursion into interior being, as at the height of Byzantine culture); (*c*) the social order; (*d*) "glorified" persons, or "thrones," each an apotheosis of a man or woman presented on the primary, or historical, stair of this four-step ladder. The phrase "state of mind" can be exchanged for "landscape of memory," a term frequently used for the last poetry of William Carlos Williams. Through imagination, the artist can resort to the physical world, which both writers so magnificently do, either when deprived of this by time or by geographic removal (as Pound was at Saint Elizabeth's). The past can be transmuted by reminiscence, just as the future can be explored by prophecy.

One of the most poignant ideas in *The Cantos* is a parenthetical comment appearing in the forty-second: "(to be young is to suffer./ Be old and be past that)." Life did not justify these words in Pound's regard; nevertheless, through art he has been able to objectify experiences, winnowing them so that they reveal an affirmative direction when viewed in totality. Besides imagination, or its related powers such as memory, books have played a large part in this discernment of immortal concepts as he reincarnated them. In his reading, he has recognized "forms" breaking through from century to century into the mortal world—unique, but having in common principles of benevolence older than Confucius and younger than Jefferson. These two need not appear in *Thrones* because Pound has already established their places in the "tale of the tribe."

Thrones requires the full attention of the reader: until it has been more widely written about, this concentration suffices for at least a modest degree of appreciation. Pound says in *Polite Essays*, speaking of the *Inferno*, "Dante wrote his poem to MAKE PEOPLE THINK." [25] In the same context, he denies that *The Divine Comedy* is obscure: "We owe Binyon [the translator] a great deal for showing us how little Dante needs NOTES." [26] Possibly, as in most editions of Dante Alighieri, Pound's epic should have explanatory or summarizing passages as headnotes, at least after the masterpiece has entered that world which Eliot calls tradition, an ideal order of artifacts. Without distorting the poetry, these introductions could well bring out the pattern of each separate Canto as well as that of the complete work.

Thrones treats several civilizations: Rome, Byzantium, China, England, showing how each contained responsible leaders concerned about the good of their fellows. Two lines from Canto 97 exemplify Pound's "enthronement" strategy: "Mons of Jute should have his name in the record, thrones, courage,/ Mons should have his name in the record." He wished to celebrate the heroism of this Briton who, unarmed, read a demand of deposition to the tyrant of Denmark, after which the latter fled like the coward that he was. Mons and others of like virtue Pound calls lights of the world ("lumina mundi" in Latin, with a rough translation from the Greek in Canto 96—"something to boast about"). The sort of "complete man" whom Pound wants for a ruler is described by Paul A. Olson:

That is, each of Pound's heroes gathers the particular facts which are important to government in his locale, the lay of the land, the crops, the feel of the people, and from these he deduces as artist-scientist the practical rules which will make his society work.[27]

The sixth-century Roman emperor Justinian the Great is a throne because of his codification of Roman Law and because he made peace with the Lombards. Among others in the imperial line singled out as thrones are Diocletian, Vespasian, Antoninus, Heraclius. In his eulogies Pound departs from Dante's brand of patriotism in that he will praise even the enemies of Rome if these are worthy rulers: men like the barbarian Authari, with his "marvelous reign, no violence, and no passports" (Canto 106).

Among its denotations the word *thrones* means a division of the paradisal choir descending from the Divinity and turning the crystal sphere encircling Jupiter. Dante's *The Divine Comedy,* prototype for Pound's *schema,* has Cunizza of the third heaven define those angels called Thrones as "mirrors reflecting the mind of God as Judge": by looking at these bright creatures, lower intelligences can see how God evaluates the works of man.[28] Beatrice, in the Crystalline Heaven, ranks the Thrones next to the Cherubim and Seraphim in the ninefold company of the celestial hierarchy.[29]

In his book-length tribute to Gaudier-Brzeska, killed in World War I, Pound compares that group of angels just below the two highest to the propositions of Descartian geometry: "The statements of 'analytics' are 'lords' over fact. They are the Thrones and Dominations that rule over form and recurrence." [30] This use is an analogy derived from a Throne as one of the most powerful of angelic spirits. Its application to structural techniques in *The Cantos* is bound in with almost everything its author himself has said on this subject.

When employed as synonym for "royal seat, chair," *throne* is related to the Latin *firmus,* itself akin to the Greek *thronos,* meaning solid, not capable of change, steadfast. Canto 97 expresses this sense graphically: "Belascio or Topaze and not have it sqush,/ a throne, something God can sit on/ without having it sqush." In Canto 98 Pound refers to light "More solid than pearls or than cassia," the latter a tree of the warm regions that formed the setting for the Old Testament narration of God's dealings with His people. Again, in Canto 104, he mentions "Topaz, God can sit on," likening the throne to a silicate occurring in white translucent masses, suggesting the giant metaphor of the crystal sphere. The entire body of medieval literature on the physics of light serves as basis for his concept.

Connected with this noun is the familiar thought that the "thrones" left vacant by the fallen angels await the arrival of men who have spent their time of pilgrimage discharging worthily the duties of their states of life: Charlemagne, Canute, Edward III, a multitude of others. To help students coming to this section of the epic for the first time Pound chooses in *Selected Cantos* parts of Cantos 99, 105, 108, and 109.

Canto 99 concerns law (in Chinese, fa^{3-5}), the people ($meng^2$), character ($tuan^1$), the last sometimes denoting principles. The title Pound gives it in his selection, "And if your kids don't study, that's your fault," originates in F. W. Baller's *The Sacred Edict:* "Instruct the Rising Generation, with a view to preventing Evil Doing"[31] Other related *dicta* are close parallels. The Canto is largely expository; yet one can discover within its pages at least nineteen lines of imagistic beauty.

The goal for Canto 105 is set in the line which Pound uses to name it: "You cannot leave things out": you cannot delete history, any more than you can fill up blank spaces of ignorance by inventing. Anselm, successor of Lanfranc, has been omitted from the education of the young, though in Pound's well-worn copy of John Richard Green's *History of the English People* he is given full credit for his contribution to Western civilization: "His famous works were the first attempts of any Christian thinker to elicit the idea of God from the very nature of the human reason." [32] Anselm went into exile rather than pay a promotion tax to Rufus, second son of William the Conqueror. Pound's admiration for him was fed during the Saint Elizabeth days through a gift from Norman Holmes Pearson of the biography by Charles Remusat. Another throne is Saint Ambrose, about whom Pound writes to the Reverend Vianney Devlin, O.F.M.: "I spect Ambrose the first bish with LARGE rents who hadn't hunted the job to get 'em." [33]

Each Canto, though not independent of the rest, has its own unity. Before dismissing the group as unpoetic, those who dislike *Thrones* (and some reviewers have been harsh) ought to look in Agassiz-fashion at the eleventh in the sequence, even though this one is not among the four containing "main elements in the Cantos." Canto 106 is the most lyrical in *Thrones*. The integrating color is gold, to correspond to its theme: the relationship between a sound economy based on grain, and the good of society. Into his vision of earthly civilization Pound draws the eternal gods: Demeter, Persephone, Artemis, Apollo, Leucothoe, together with half-divine beings who illuminate transitory scenes. The opening five lines of the Canto constitute a metrically perfect song:

> And was her daughter like that;
> Black as Demeter's gown,
>   eyes, hair?
> Dis' bride, Queen over Phlegethon,   [cf. Canto 75]
>   girls faint as mist about her?

The two end-rhymes (*gown, Phlegethon*) are picked up later in lines seven and eight with *grain* and *Kuan*. Alliterated key words enhance the effectiveness of the sound-pattern.

The mythological figures of Canto 106 belong to the allegorical upper level of the Schifanoia frescoes by Cosimo Tura: most noteworthy among them is that positive force, Demeter, the goddess of harvest and fruitfulness. She was not only the mother of Persephone but also the mother by Jason of Plutus, god of wealth. Disguised as an old woman, she went all over the world seeking her daughter after the rape of the girl by Dis, until compassionate Apollo revealed Persephone's place of concealment, among the ghosts of Hades. Persephone's fate is described thus by William Sherwood Fox:

Persephone, the daughter of Demeter by Zeus, was playing in the meadows of Nysia with nymphs of the sea and plucking the wild flowers of the springtime—roses, crocuses, irises, violets and hyacinths—when she spied an especially beautiful and fragrant stalk of narcissus and hastened to pick it.[34]

When Persephone reached for the blossom, the earth cracked open and the King of Hell (father of the Furies as well) swept her away to his bleak home, where only the asphodel blooms.[35] Paralleling Pound's tendency to telescope characters, Fox combines Persephone and Demeter, a practice he says was followed until the fourth century.[36] Frazer's *Golden Bough* goes even further by identifying this myth of death and rebirth with those of Aphrodite and Adonis, Cybele and Attis, Isis and Osiris.[37] The black shawl still capitalized on by Venetian merchants is accounted for thus by Fox: he pictures Demeter "with her yellow tresses veiled in a dark mourning mantle," [38] as she seeks Persephone over land and sea. The whole story prefigures Easter:

Above all, the thought of the seed buried in the earth in order to spring up to new and higher life readily suggested a comparison with human destiny, and strengthened the hope that for man too the grave may be but the beginning of a better and happier existence in some brighter world unknown.[39]

Although such numinous references connect the mundane with the universal, Pound primarily employs the Persephone cycle to show that the strength of men, as he says in line six of this Canto, is in grain.

Later in the Canto the poet returns to the daughter of Demeter, quoting (perhaps from himself): " 'Venice shawls from Demeter's gown,' " and then strangely combining the Mediterranean world with the state of Virginia, site of family connections ("Persephone in the cotton-field"). The mythic substructure persists in

> this is grain rite
> near Enna, at Nyssa:
> Circe, Persephone
> so different is sea from glen that
> the juniper is her holy bush

Enna was the city of Sicily near where the abduction occurred. Pound knows that he cannot keep readers engaged with catalogues of historical items alone. He needs the contrast which Olympian music and Botticellian designs provide. Persephone has all along been a leading character, a figure of his daughter, Mary, a resemblance which returns us to our human world of sighs and joy.

In Canto 106, Yao and Shun, Chinese emperors who ruled by jade, reappear; so does the seventh-century B.C. Kuan Chung, who taught his contemporaries how to govern. Beyond the reach of the common sense which they represent exists the beauty of Helen; of Apeliota, the southeast wind; of the six deities framing his prayer in need to Diana.

In this Canto, the only point at which an autobiographical note might be necessary is "Luigi in the hill path/ this is grain rite." Yet what difference does it make whether a specific Luigi is meant? A century from now, all but two or three lines of this Canto will be granted poeticity by every reader, especially the exquisite

> So slow is the rose to open.
> A match flares in the eyes' hearth,
>   then darkness.

The "heavy transformations of the light" nowhere show themselves more active than in Pound's images of the river of fire, Phlegethon; "the gold light of wheat surging upward/ ungathered"; the sunset reflected on the Amazon and Orinoco; the Ko Lu river gold destined for coining; the hypostasis "That the goddess turn crystal within her" (in other words, that love become as immortal as its personification, Venus). In the spirit of the oft-repeated line about beauty living in the mind of Artemis he uses his poem to enthrone many while at the same time reserving the highest honors to "that Venere," who when she departs leaves behind her an empty house (Canto 106).

The last two Cantos in *Thrones* which Pound sees as requisite points of entrance are 108 and 109. The first dwells on English jurisprudence. By his implied praise of the fourteenth-century Edward III, of Queen Elizabeth, of Sir Edward Coke, he avoids in his own person the crime here referred to as "souls of the dead defrauded." One gets an impression of responsibility in places of power, care for the small landholder, scrupulous honesty guided by "Angliae amor." England is, after all, the land of his forebears.

As Pound moves into the next Canto, the principle of beauty is incarnated in bird, flower, light, mountain:

> Wing like feldspar
> and the foot-grip firm to hold balance
> Green yellow the sunlight, more rapid,
> Azaleas by snow slope.

The mineral feldspar can be crystalline white or flesh-red: therefore, the color of the wing here might echo the snowy peak, or it might stand out in brilliant contrast. Thrones in Canto 109 are Edward, Duke of Windsor, who earned that designation before he abdicated; Erigena; Anselm. In 1956, Pound remarks to Father Vianney Devlin in a letter: "Giovannini not finding Chas Remusat's life of St. Anselm in Wash." [40] Eventually, as has been said above, the book came to him from Yale. He concludes with churches like the Roman San Domenico and Santa Sabina, about which he once wrote Denis Goacher that they, being romanistic, belonged to his "line" rather than the gothic Chartres.[41]

To the glory of these mortal thrones is added the figure of Helios. Then Pound's own handbook to *The Cantos* ends with his translation of the *Paradiso*, II, 1: "You in the dinghey (piccioletta) astern there!" On the note of this sharp bidding, "Pay attention!" he leaves the reader on his own to voyage through the last Cantos of the *periplum*.

Pound's acclamation of Leo Frobenius is well known. Anthropology fascinated him, not only African but also Chinese, especially the scientific prose of Joseph F. Rock, who is the dominating influence in Canto 110.[42] By combining the words for *wind, tiger, oak,* and *five,* a Tibetan tribe had long ago named their ceremony devised to free spirits in bondage to the [2] Mun 'ghügh demons.[43] Nowhere in *The Cantos* is Pound more lyrical, the verses recalling his Noh translation wherein Kakitsubata, Spirit of the Iris, recites:

> The lightfoot summer comes nigh us,
> The branching trees and the bright unmindful grass
> Do not forget their time,
> They take no thought, yet remember
> To show forth their colour in season.[44]

The connection between Professor Rock and the Japanese drama lies in the fact that the jealous Hannya of the latter can be overcome only by exorcism. At the conclusion of Canto 110, Pound refers to Awoi, Flower of the East, the heroine of the Noh play. Purification continues to be the theme as details of the sacrifice are explored. The Indian cosmography summoned up by reference to Mt. Sumeru, the world's axis, recalls Yeats's symbolic vision.

Pound now returns to a line of Canto 106, "And in thy mind beauty, O Artemis," knowing that he cannot surpass it.

Dove sta memoria he is back at Sirmione, where willow and olive are reflected in a lake which is one shade of blue while the sky is another.

Though Canto 111 remains incomplete and unpolished, it is precious for such lines as

> Amor
> Gold mermaid up from black water—
> Night against sea-cliffs
> the low reef of coral—
> And the sea grey against undertow

all of which returns us to the Ovidian magic of the second Canto. In Canto 112, Pound summons back the ² Muàn ¹ bpö ceremony, as well as that analogue of Mount Taishan the snow range Li Chiang. Canto 113 advances the epic in that it begins with the all-pervasive sun (opposed to temporality as this is figured by the moon), this time in the form of the charioteer Phoebus Apollo; Helios travels through the zodiac of the Cosimo Tura fresco, alternating joy and pain like the Goddess Fortuna ("tasting the sweet and the sorry").

Despite the threnody which *Drafts & Fragments* really is, its composer is still able to walk in imagination through a garden where his companions are the great precisionists Mozart, Agassiz, Linnaeus. Even yet, China around the Li Chiang range ("a thin trace in blue air") is accessible to him in quiet retreats where old friends (H.D.) return to share his solitude. Music and light are present in these Cantos ("the snow range is turquoise," "a clear wind over garofani," "grass versus granite,/ For the little light and more harmony," "In mountain air the grass frozen emerald," "A blue light under stars," "Daphne afoot in vain speed"). Yet hope and despair hold hands: "Out of dark, thou, Father Helios, leadest,/ but the mind as Ixion, unstill, ever turning." Goethe's devil was right in telling Faust that hell was within him; at the same time, Mephistopheles gains no victory over the hero.

In quoting Voltaire's statement that he hates no one, not even Fréron, Pound in Canto 114 intends us by extension to recognize his own benevolence. In his mid-thirties he had written: "I have no hatred. To the best of my knowledge I have no prejudice, and I have never consciously 'abused' the land of my birth." [45] In his sixties he was charged with such abuse and never able to dissociate himself from the unfavorable publicity which often convicted him without trial. Living abroad in obscurity he quietly writes down once more in these fragmentary Cantos his lifelong belief in Love, central to Dante's poem and his own.

Strong ties unite Botticelli and Ezra Pound from the first to latest poems: in Canto 114 the poet explicitly links the *Quattrocento* painters with verbal art, finding in them the true narrative and lyric poetry of their day: "And the literature of his time (Sandro's, Firenze) was in painting." In "Gems sunned as mirrors, alternate" he pays tribute to another art of the Renaissance, the goldsmith's—such a necklace Simonetta might have worn.

As octogenarian, Pound transcends any hurry or scurry beneath the changing moon, a motif which has for him as much depth as for any tragic protagonist of the *de casibus* tradition. Now retrospective, he has little desire to castigate; rather would he crown with begemmed light the men and women who have meant most to him, in history and within his own family or circle of friends. These occupy their thrones in the realm of his thought without any competition:

> ubi amor, ibi oculus.
> But these had thrones,
>   and in my mind were still, uncontending—
> not to possession, in hypostasis
>   Some hall of mirrors.

In Pisa he descended the supreme *bolge* of sorrow; as he made the perilous ascent after his release from the D.T.C. he learned the value of kindness: "And that the truth is in kindness."

Toward life's end, Pound wrestles with self-doubt. He knows what every artist must finally admit: one cannot write Paradise. But the cosmos coheres, beyond any transcript. All of that which is durable in classical literature, East and West, as he has encountered it, all of his own visions and revisions have gone into *The Cantos* as palimpsest. The "erasures" are not really that: their originals still exist under new and newer beauty. The words are done in gold light on the newest surface of the palimpsest—modest, as things human must necessarily be: "A little light, like a rushlight/ to lead back to splendour." More and more personal as they proceed, the Cantos after the hundredth frequently echo a sense of failure, "a tangle of works unfinished." Pound's humility, the direct opposite of hybris, sees far less in his total achievement than is really there; or perhaps one might say that with authentic sensitivity he judges even the highest masterpiece of man to be only "a rushlight."

Pound's final rounding off of the "crystal sphere" metaphor

has been immediately anticipated by that of thrones. The pearl beyond price, which has been foreshadowed in phenomena, is made perfect in imagination:

> In this sphere is Giustizia.
> In mountain air the grass frozen emerald
> and with the mind set on that light
> saffron, emerald,
> seeping (Canto 113)

Much as he depreciated the Old Testament approach to man's relationship with God, Pound was thoroughly familiar with it from his Presbyterian upbringing, from which he did not detach himself until he became an expatriate. Gerhard von Rad connects these two concepts of throne and sphere in the first volume of his *Old Testament Theology:* "To the Israelite, on the contrary, 'justice' is often understood in an oddly spatial way, 'as something like a sphere, or power-charged area, into which men are incorporated and thereby empowered to do special deeds.' " [46] Grace begins on earth and ends in glory. Leaders such as Mons of Jute are already thrones before their entrance into the eternal sphere. It is this crystal sphere, introduced in youthful lyrics and an entire career in the building, which acts as the central unifying image of *The Cantos.*

Since the time that Pound made his selection of vital passages, *Drafts & Fragments of Cantos CX-CXVII* has appeared. For the sake of completeness, publisher James Laughlin has added to *Selected Cantos of Ezra Pound* the unfinished poems called Cantos 115 and 116. Light, as earlier in the work, is equated with the eternal. In the gloom it may seem only "a pale flare over marshes," but it lasts beyond the flourishing of the salt hay, beyond even Neptune, from whom all life rises in his personification of the sea. Hercules in the Sophoclean play translated by Pound found death the great goal—not so here; there is something beyond, something consequent upon the "blown husk that is finished." Though blackness exists, so does eternal beauty.

The fragment of Canto 115 which constitutes the New Directions selection differs significantly from the version Eva Hesse included in *Ezra Pound: Cantos 1916–1962,* which begins:

> The gold thread in the dark pattern at Torcello.
> The wall still stands.
>> There is a path by a field almost empty.
> Great trees over an avenue

It would seem that three locations are united here, all rich with a light thrown over them by memory. The following two lines coincide in both editions. Then the newer introduces "Mozart, Linnaeus, Sulmona" before it repeats the three lines of Miss Hesse's fragment. It omits the next seven lines, most of which occur elsewhere, and concludes with the same words as the earlier version. Such changes prepare for Pound's use, in the following draft, of the noun *palimpsest* to clarify the nature of his text.

The first two pages of the expanded New Directions excerpts list under "Addendum for Canto C" a lyric which was originally part of Canto 72 as published in the magazine *Vice Versa* for January, 1942, ten lines of it having been sent to Katue Kitasono in 1940. The rest of the addition to the hundredth Canto begins with a simplification of Chaucer's "And the yonge sonne/ Hath in the Ram his halve course yronne":

"Now sun rises in Ram sign." This is followed by the freshness of Rapallo in springtime with bright rocks of the mountain path petaled by the shadows of water-bugs; cherry blossoms; the carillon of Saint Panteleon playing Mozart; birds
singing a Jannequin motet; and all around San Ambrogia the
olive trees awakening.

Some critics affirm that such exquisite interludes as these,
woven haphazardly into what they consider an unpoetic fab-
ric, are the only valuable portions of *The Cantos*, that the
whole thing is merely "drafts and fragments." Not so George
T. Wright, who after making a study of point of view in the
poem concludes:

The "I" is its presenter, its singer; the poem is his song, his monument. Yet even while the persona wanders among his memories,
we feel the presence of a still fuller intelligence superintending the
wandering. We feel the poet in his poem as the singing persona,
but we also feel him behind the poem's pattern as the composer of
this enormous song. There is point in all the random memories,
order in all the apparent meandering.[47]

He who looks for excellences, such as a unifying thread, has a
better chance of discovery than he who pre-judges on the
basis of secondary sources. Neither envious nor egotistical,
Pound finds it hard to see why readers cannot entertain
perfections objectively, why they must find in them the seeds
of a storm such as that conveyed by the thunder ideogram
stamped on the back cover of *Thrones*. All he asks is openness to the poetry as such.

Had Dante lived beyond the traditional span allotted to
man, *his* narrative vision might have trembled in his own es-
timation, even as Pound's has. Amidst uncertainties on the

part of the author, the American's dream continues to ascend, propelled more by suffering than by joy through the final spiraling stages. Life itself is jeopardy, as poet Jack Gilbert stresses in the title of his volume in the Yale Series of Younger Poets; assuredly it is perilous, especially when not only "examined" but transformed into an all-encompassing art-form.

The notes intended for a future Canto 117 (and more beyond) act not only as a summary of Pound's autobiography but also as his epitaph. He gives thanks for the blessings of this earth: "For the blue flash and the moments/ benedetta" (perhaps a recollection of when he sat with Cummings under the trees of Saint Elizabeth's) and for

> Brancusi's bird
> in the hollow of pine trunks
> or when the snow was like sea foam
> Twilit sky leaded with elm boughs.

Zagreus (E.P.) someday expects to have his "altar," when jealousies are long dead: light will pour in from "the double arch of a window" across its circle of worship. Even now, he speaks as if from Olympus, pleading with the world "To be men not destroyers."

On the last page of *The Cantos* Pound writes of how he has tried "to make a paradise/ terrestre." Paradise can never be put into words. But to try is a high enterprise—for a poet, the highest.

Epilogue

Perhaps some day, as Eustace Mullins has predicted, Pound will win the Nobel Prize; [1] so Hemingway hoped and so many others have hoped. His poetry is becoming more and more appreciated. James Laughlin of New Directions has faithfully kept it in print. The "better maker" has had disciples but never an impresario. In his old age, unconcerned about honors, he lives quietly, sustained by the permanence exsiting underneath the passing—lives according to his own "What thou lovest well remains,/ the rest is dross." This promise from Canto 81 safeguards public, not merely personal, good. His country's debt to its greatest living poet will be paid, little by little, by the ages, if it is not paid in our own century by us.

Notes

CHAPTER 1   EZRA POUND THE MAN

1. "Pound and the Poetry of Perception," *Thought*, XXXV (Autumn 1960), 340.

2. *The Poetry of Ezra Pound*, p. 5.

3. Manuscript Collection of the Philadelphia Free Library.

4. *Ibid.* Photographs preserved in this collection record this period in Pound's education. They were donated by his former teacher Mr. Doolittle.

5. In 1967 Miss Warren, past ninety but still alert, related to me her reminiscences of those days. The interview took place in a Lutheran nursing home in Wyncote.

6. *The Letters of Ezra Pound, 1907–1941*. The entire group from which the selection was made after Mr. and Mrs. Paige returned from going through the Rapallo files reposes in the Beinecke Rare Book and Manuscript Collection at Yale University, abbreviated throughout this volume as YALC (Yale American Literature Collection). Almost ten times as many letters exist there in the Paige transcripts as have been printed. Many more are contained in the Pound Archives, as yet unavailable for examination by scholars.

7. These can be consulted in Hamilton's Treasure Room, which, under the direction of Mrs. Betty Wallace, has been developed into as fine a source of Poundiana as exists in this country. Almost all the items listed in Donald C. Gallup's excellent bibliography are available there, in addition to a large bulk of correspondence with James Taylor Dunn, Cyril Clemens (of the Mark Twain Museum in Hannibal), and Joseph Ibbotson. Pound himself has been a generous donor.

8. *Books and Their Makers during the Middle Ages.*

9. February, 1905, YALC.

10. Letter to author, July 31, 1969.

11. Noel Stock, *The Life of Ezra Pound*, p. 44. Detailed biographical information on the poet can be found here, as well as in the books by Charles Norman and others.

12. *Poetry in Our Time*, p. 122.

13. February 21, 1909, YALC.

14. December 5, 1909, YALC.

15. *Ibid.* In his sardonic self-depreciation here, he seems to anticipate the judgment of Robert Graves, who in the December, 1957, issue of *Esquire* (p. 8, letter to the editor) asserts that since 1912 he has been insisting that Pound is not even a good poet, let alone a great one.

16. Cf. the collection in Hamilton College's Treasure Room.

17. May, 1911, YALC.

18. February 26, 1912, YALC.

19. Harry Meacham, *The Caged Panther*, p. 16.

20. P. 46.   21. *Writers at Work*, II, 21.

22. *Ibid.*, p. 22.   23. February 22, 1914, YALC.

24. April 12, 1914, YALC. Despite Noel Stock's assertion in *The Life of Ezra Pound* (p. 154), Pound had informed his parents as to the exact date, although this letter may not have reached the Wyncote household before the *Philadelphia Inquirer* item was submitted. Stock himself mentions the formal invitation received in early April.

25. Letter to Homer L. Pound, summer of 1922, YALC.

26. October, 1916, YALC.

27. *Selected Letters of E. E. Cummings*, edited by F. W. Dupee and George Stade, p. 79.

28. "Pound in Exile," *Intro*, I (1951), 165.

29. January 21, 1931, YALC.

30. October, 1908 (Paige, *The Letters of Ezra Pound*, p. 5).

31. November 6, 1936, YALC.

32. *The Life of Ezra Pound*, p. 314.

33. Rare Book and Manuscript Collection of the University of Texas in Austin, Texas.

34. *New England Quarterly*, March, 1948, p. 11.

35. Gatter correspondence, April, 1958, Manuscript Collection of the Philadelphia Free Library.

36. *Accademia Bulletin*, No. 2, Washington, D.C.

37. *New Republic*, June 7, 1969, p. 25.

38. *Selected Letters of E. E. Cummings*, p. 259.

39. *Ibid.*, p. 104.   40. *Ibid.*, p. 125.

41. *Ibid.*, p. 115. 42. *Ibid.*, p. 135.
43. *Ibid.*, p. 161. 44. *Ibid.*, p. 176.
45. *Ibid.*, p. 189. 46. *Ibid.*, p. 196.
47. *Ibid.*, p. 217. 48. *Ibid.*, p. 218.
49. *Ibid.*, p. 249. 50. *Ibid.*, p. 230.
51. *Ibid.*, p. 249. 52. *Ibid.*, p. 254.
53. *Ibid.*, pp. 255–256. 54. *Ibid.*, p. 273.
55. *Ibid.*, p. 274. 56. Letter to author, 1969.

CHAPTER 2 THE POET AS PRECEPTOR

1. *The Literary Essays of Ezra Pound*, p. x.
2. *Ibid.*, p. xi. 3. *Ibid.*, p. xiii.
4. November 22, 1968, p. 96. 5. *Ibid.*
6. *The Literary Essays of Ezra Pound*, pp. 74–75.
7. *Ibid.*, p. 78. 8. *Ibid.*, p. 80. 9. P. 7.
10. *The Poetry of Ezra Pound*, p. 117.
11. P. 13. 12. P. 14.
13. P. 30. 14. P. 58.
15. *Selected Cantos of Ezra Pound*, p. 9.
16. Rare Book Collection, University of Texas, Austin, Texas.
17. *ABC of Reading*, p. 34.
18. *The Literary Essays of Ezra Pound*, p. 59.
19. *Ibid.*, p. 62.
20. *The Egoist*, March 16, 1914, p. 108.
21. *Gaudier-Brzeska*, p. 97. 22. *Ibid.*
23. *Ibid.*, p. 99. 24. *Ibid.*, p. 102.
25. *Ibid.*, p. 106. 26. *Ibid.*, p. 107.
27. *Ibid.*, p. 136. 28. *Ibid.*, p. 147.
29. *Vision Fugitive: Ezra Pound and Economics*, p. 202.
30. Rare Book and Manuscript Collection, Free Library of Philadelphia.
31. Rare Book Collection, University of Texas, Austin, Texas.
32. *The Poetry of Ezra Pound*, p. 7.
33. P. xii. 34. P. 44.
35. *The Spirit of Romance*, p. 7. 36. *Ibid.*, p. 8.
37. Jacob Burckhardt. *The Civilization of the Renaissance in Italy and Other Selections*, ed. Alexander Dru, p. 233.
38. *Confucius to Cummings: An Anthology of Poetry*, p. 8.
39. *Ibid.*, pp. 86–88. 40. *Ibid.*, p. 335.
41. *Ibid.*, p. 322. 42. *Ibid.*, p. 340.

CHAPTER 3   POUND'S EARLY LYRICS

1. The lyrics explicated in Chapter 3 are from this book.
2. *The Troubadours,* p. 11.   3. P. 198.
4. *The Early Poetry of Ezra Pound,* p. 33.
5. *Ezra Pound: The Image and the Real,* p. 6.
6. *Fortnightly Review,* September 1, 1914, p. 46.
7. P. 64 ("The Prose Tradition in Verse").
8. *Poetry in Our Time,* p. 123.   9. P. 341.
10. Deutsch, *Poetry in Our Time,* p. 122.
11. *Selected Poems,* p. 11.
12. Herbert Schneidau, *Ezra Pound: The Image and the Real,* p. 36.
This book explores to a highly useful degree the Jamesian analogue.

CHAPTER 4   POUND'S BOOK OF CHANGES

1. *The Odyssey,* p. 187. The other Book XI citations from Robert
Fitzgerald's version directly follow.
2. *The Poetry of Ezra Pound,* p. 25.
3. Paige, *The Letters of Ezra Pound,* p. 91.
4. *Polite Essays,* p. 173.   5. *Ibid.,* p. 104.
6. Paige, *The Letters of Ezra Pound,* p. 230.
72. Only seven of the twelve translations from Propertius appear in
Selected Poems of Ezra Pound: I, III, IV, VI, VII, IX, XII.
8. Paige, *The Letters of Ezra Pound,* p. 181.
9. *Ibid.,* p. 175.   10. *Sailing after Knowledge,* p. 147.
11. *Sex. Propertii Elegia,* p. 63.
12. Paige, *The Letters of Ezra Pound,* p. 150.
13. P. 127.   14. Paige, *The Letters of Ezra Pound,* p. 91.
15. *ABC of Reading,* p. 48.
16. *Ezra Pound and Sextus Propertius,* p. 76.   17. P. 48.
18. *The Poetry of Ezra Pound,* p. 25.
19. *The Earliest English Poetry,* p. 111.
20. *Anglo-Saxon Poetry,* p. 84.
21. *The Translations of Ezra Pound,* p. 20.
22. Pp. 19–20.   23. *Anglo-Saxon Poetry,* p. 84.
24. *Ibid.,* p. 86.   25. *Ibid.*
26. *The Earliest English Poetry,* p. 113.
27. James R. Hulbert, ed., *Bright's Anglo-Saxon Reader,* p. cvi.
28. Paige, *The Letters of Ezra Pound,* p. 293.

29. *Ibid.*, p. 8.   30. P. 8.

31. Referred to in several of the John Quinn letters, Manuscript Collection, New York Public Library.

32. Pp. 56–57.

33. Rare Book Collection, University of Texas, Austin.

34. This likeness will be developed at length in a future essay by me on Ezra Pound.

35. "For a New Paideuma," *The Criterion*, XVIII (January, 1938), 208.

36. Paige, *The Letters of Ezra Pound*, p. 27.

37. *The Reporter*, XXXVII (November 2, 1967), 60.

38. *Pharos*, I (Winter, 1947), 28.

39. "Ezra Pound as a Translator of Classical Chinese Poetry," *Sewanee Review*, XXXIII (Summer, 1965), 351.

40. *Writers at Work*, II, 56.

41. *The Art of Reading*, p. 147.   42. P. 207.

CHAPTER 5   THE CANTOS: FROM EREBUS TO PISA

1. YALC.

2. Paige, *The Letters of Ezra Pound*, p. 239.

3. Published in London by Faber & Faber.

4. *The New Age*, March 7, 1918, p. 378.

5. John Addington Symonds, *The Age of the Despots*, p. 134. That Pound knew and approved of Symonds is clear from the fact that as foreign editor of *The Little Review* he brought out a play by him.

6. *Ibid.*, p. 135.   7. *Ibid.*   8. P. 23.

9. Symonds, *The Age of the Despots*, p. 89.

10. Noel Stock, *The Life of Ezra Pound*, p. 176.

11. Paige, *The Letters of Ezra Pound*, p. 239.

12. Letter to John Lackay Brown, April, 1937, YALC.

13. *Ezra Pound: A Close-up*, p. 52.

14. These books were edited by Andrew A. Lipscomb for the Thomas Jefferson Memorial Association, Washington, D.C., in 1905.

15. *Writings of Thomas Jefferson*, XIV, 5.

16. *Ibid.*, p. 386 (January 9, 1816).

17. Number 9 out of an edition of 300, with a foreword by Olga Rudge.

18. P. 53.   19. *Paradiso*, XIX, 118.

20. September 29, 1936, YALC.

21. *The Life of Ezra Pound*, p. 328.

22. *Poetry in Our Time*, p. 127.

23. Couvreur's translation was published in Hokien in 1913 by Imprimerie de la Mission Catholique.

24. August 25, 1940, YALC.

25. April 19, 1970.

CHAPTER 6 THE CANTOS: THE PERILOUS ASCENT

1. *The Trial of Ezra Pound*, p. 20.

2. November–December, 1961 (Boston).

3. See chapter 1, n. 15.

4. *Pound/Joyce*, p. 275.

5. *Benjamin Minor;* tr. S. V. Yankowski, p. 83.

6. *Conceptions of Reality in Modern American Poetry*, p. 174.

7. P. ix.

8. Cf. the article "Mr. Epstein and the Critics" by T. E. Hulme, in *The New Age*, XIV (December 25, 1913), 251–53, for a reproduction of "The Rock Drill."

9. Noel Stock, ed., *Ezra Pound Perspectives: Essays in Honor of His Eightieth Birthday*, p. 198.

10. *Ibid.*   11. P. 40.

12. All of Pound's ideograms are contained in his heavily marked *A Chinese-English Dictionary*, compiled by R. H. Mathews in 1931.

13. P. 343.

14. *Ezra Pound: Poet as Sculptor*, p. 206.

15. *Chou King*, pp. 337–38.

16. *The British Union Quarterly*, January–April, 1937, p. 40.

17. *The Continuity of American Poetry*, p. 99. Pearce's view strikes me as more valid than Noel Stock's statement: "The eleven *Rock-Drill* cantos do not form a whole or connect in any way with other sections." *The Life of Ezra Pound*, p. 439.

18. P. 154.

19. *Reading the Cantos*, p. 97.

20. December, 1935, YALC.

21. Book V, l. 344.

22. *Ideas into Action: A Study of Pound's Cantos*, p. 117.

23. XXI, 25.

24. *Writers at Work*, II, 58.

25. *Polite Essays*, p. 33.   26. *Ibid.*, p. 38.

27. "Pound and the Poetry of Perception," *Thought*, XXXV (Autumn, 1960), 341.

28. *Paradiso*, IX, 61–62.

29. *Ibid.*, XXVIII, 104–5.

30. *Gaudier-Brzeska*, p. 106.   31. P. 119.

32. Vol. I, p. 101. The book was part of the poet's boyhood: his copy is inscribed to his maternal grandmother in the year of its publication, 1822.

33. June 1í 1956, YALC.

34. *The Mythology of All Races*, I, 227.

35. G. M. Kirkwood, in *A Short Guide to Classical Mythology*, writes about the land of Dis: "It is a gloomy, dark, and barren region, its only vegetation the weed asphodel" (p. 43).

36. *The Mythology of All Races*, I, 232.

37. *Spirits of the Corn and of the Wild*, p. 35.

38. *The Mythology of All Races*, I, 36.

39. Frazer, *Spirits of the Corn and of the Wild*, p. 90.

40. October 20, 1956, YALC.

41. The Berg Collection of the New York Public Library (August 11, 1953).

42. Rock's lengthy "The ² Muan ¹ Bpö Ceremony—or the Sacrifice to Heaven as Practiced by the ¹Na-²khi," *Monumenta Serica*, XIII (1948), 1–160, is the source-treatise used here.

43. *Ibid.*, p. 65, n. 163.

44. *The Translations of Ezra Pound*, p. 333.

45. "The Regional," *The New Age*, XXV (June 12, 1919), 124.

46. P. 376.

47. *The Poet in the Poem: The Personae of Eliot, Yeats, and Pound*, p. 157.

EPILOGUE

1. *This Difficult Individual*, p. 280.

Bibliography

WORKS BY EZRA POUND

ABC of Reading. New York: New Directions, 1960.

A Lume Spento and Other Early Poems. New York: New Directions, 1965. Originally published in 1908, for the author, by A. Antonini, Venice.

Antheil and the Treatise on Harmony. Paris: Three Mountains Press, 1924.

Canto CX. Cambridge, Mass.: As Sextant Press, 1965.

"Canto Proceeding (72 Circa)," *Vice Versa,* Vol. I (January, 1942), front cover.

The Cantos (1–95). New York: New Directions, 1956.

[Confucius.] *The Unwobbling Pivot & The Great Digest,* tr. *Pharos,* I (Winter, 1947), 5–53.

Confucius to Cummings: An Anthology of Poetry. Ed. with Marcella Spann. New York: New Directions, 1964.

"Demarcations," *The British Union Quarterly,* January–April, 1937, pp. 35–41.

A Draft of XVI Cantos. Paris: Three Mountains Press, 1928.

Drafts & Fragments of Cantos CX–CXVII. New York: New Directions, 1968.

Ezra Pound: Cantos 1916–1962. Tr. and ed. by Eva Hesse. Munich: Deutscher Taschenbuch Verlag, 1964.

"For a New Paideuma," *The Criterion,* XVII (January, 1938), 205–18.

Gaudier-Brzeska: A Memoir by Ezra Pound. London: Laidlaw & Laidlaw, n.d.

Guide to Kulchur. Norfolk, Conn.: New Directions, 1952.

Hugh Selwyn Mauberley. London: The Ovid Press, 1920.

Indiscretions; or, Une Revue de Deux Mondes. Paris: Three Mountains Press, 1923.

Instigations. New York: Boni & Liveright, Publishers, 1920.

Jefferson and/or Mussolini. New York: Liveright Publishing Company, 1935.

Letters and photographs in Carl and Elsie Gatter Collection, Rare Book Room, Free Library of Philadelphia.

The Letters of Ezra Pound, 1907–1941. Ed. by D. D. Paige. New York: Harcourt, Brace and Company, 1950.

Letters to John Quinn. Manuscript Collection, New York Public Library.

Letters to various correspondents; broadcasts over Italian radio. Rare Book Collection, University of Texas Library, Austin, Texas.

Letters to various correspondents. Beinecke Rare Book and Manuscript Collection, Yale University, New Haven, Connecticut.

The Literary Essays of Ezra Pound. Ed. with an introduction by T. S. Eliot. Norfolk, Conn.: New Directions, 1954.

Love Poems of Ancient Egypt. Tr. with Noel Stock. New York: New Directions, 1962.

Lustra of Ezra Pound with Earlier Poems. New York: Privately printed, 1916.

Make It New. London: Faber & Faber, 1934.

Patria Mia. Chicago: Ralph Fletcher, 1950.

Pavannes and Divagations. New York: New Directions, 1958.

Personae. New York: Liveright Publishing Company, 1926.

Poems, 1918–1921 Including Three Portraits and Four Cantos. New York: Boni & Liveright, 1921.

Polite Essays. Freeport, N.Y.: Books for Libraries, Inc., 1966. Originally published by Faber & Faber, London, 1937.

Profile: An Anthology Collected in MCMXXXI. Milan, 1932.

Provença; Poems Selected from Personae, Exultations, and Canzoniere of Ezra Pound. Boston: Small and Maynard, 1910.

Selected Cantos of Ezra Pound. London: Faber & Faber, 1967.

Selected Cantos of Ezra Pound. New York: New Directions, 1970.

Selected Poems of Ezra Pound. Ed. by T. S. Eliot. London: Faber & Faber, 1927.

Selected Poems of Ezra Pound. New York: New Directions, 1959.

[Sophocles.] *Women of Trachis,* tr. New York: New Directions, 1957.

The Spirit of Romance. Norfolk, Conn.: New Directions, 1952.

[Ta Hio.] *The Great Learning,* tr. Seattle, Wash.: University of Washington Book Store, 1928.

Thrones: 96–109 de los Cantares. New York: New Directions, 1959.
The Translations of Ezra Pound. With an introduction by Hugh Kenner. New York: New Directions, 1953.

SECONDARY SOURCES

Baller, F. W. *The Sacred Edict.* 2nd ed. Shanghai: American Presbyterian Mission Press, 1907.

Bertoni, Giulio. *I Trovatori D'Italia.* Modena: Editore Cav. Umberto Orlandini, 1915.

Blackburn, Paul, tr. *Proensa.* Divers Press, 1953.

Briffault, Robert S. *The Troubadours.* Bloomington: Indiana University Press, 1965.

Burckhardt, Jacob. *The Civilization of the Renaissance in Italy and Other Selections.* Ed. by Alexander Dru. New York: Washington Square Press, Inc. 1966.

Cornell, Julien. *The Trial of Ezra Pound.* New York: The John Day Company, 1966.

Couvreur, S., tr. *The Book of Rites.* Ho Kien Fu: Imprimerie de la Mission Catholique, 1913.

——*Chou King.* Sien Hsien: Imprimerie de la Mission Catholique, 1934.

Cummings, E. E. *Six Non-Lectures.* Cambridge, Mass.: Harvard University Press, 1953.

Davie, Donald. *Ezra Pound: Poet as Sculptor.* New York: Oxford University Press, 1964.

Davis, Earle. *Vision Fugitive: Ezra Pound and Economics.* Lawrence: The University of Kansas Press, 1968.

Dekker, George. *Sailing after Knowledge.* London: Routledge & Kegan Paul, 1963.

Dembo, Lawrence. *Conceptions of Reality in Modern American Poetry.* Berkeley: University of California Press, 1965.

Deutsch, Babette. *Poetry in Our Time.* New York: Henry Holt and Company, 1952.

Dupee, F. W., and George Stade, eds. *Selected Letters of E. E. Cummings.* New York: Harcourt, Brace and World, Inc., 1969.

Emery, Clark. *Ideas into Action: A Study of Pound's Cantos.* Coral Gables, Fla.: University of Miami Press, 1958.

Epstein, Joseph. "The Small-eyed Poet," *New Republic,* CLX (June 7, 1969), 23–28.

Fox, William Sherwood. *Greek and Roman Mythology.* Vol. I of *The Mythology of All Races.* Boston: Marshall Jones Company, 1916.

Frazer, Sir George. *Spirits of the Corn and of the Wild.* London: Macmillan and Co., Ltd., 1914. Vols. VII and VIII of *The Golden Bough.*

Giovannini, Giovanni. *Ezra Pound and Dante.* Utrecht: Dekker & Van de Vegt N. W. Nymegen, 1961.

Goacher, Denis. "The Critics and the Master," *The Europeans,* XV (May, 1954), 24–38.

Goodwin, Kenneth. *The Influence of Ezra Pound.* London: Oxford University Press, 1966.

Gordon, R. K., tr. *Anglo-Saxon Poetry.* New York: E. P. Dutton and Co., n.d.

Green, John Richard. *History of the English People.* 2 vols. London: Wm. L. Allison & Son, 1882.

Hatfield, J. A. *Dreams and Nightmares.* Baltimore: Penguin Books, 1967.

Hénault, Marie, ed. *Studies in the Cantos,* Columbus, Ohio: Charles E. Merrill Publishing Company, 1971.

Hill, Raymond T., and Thomas G. Bergen, eds. *Anthology of the Provençal Troubadours.* New Haven: Yale University Press, 1941.

Hoffman, Daniel. "Old Ez and Uncle William," *The Reporter,* XXXVII (November 2, 1967), 59–63.

Holder, Alan. *Three Voyagers in Search of Europe: A Study of Henry James, Ezra Pound, and T. S. Eliot.* Philadelphia: University of Pennsylvania Press, 1966.

Homer. *The Odyssey.* Tr. by Robert Fitzgerald. Garden City, N.Y.: Doubleday and Company, Inc., 1963.

Hulbert, James R., ed. *Bright's Anglo-Saxon Reader.* New York: Henry Holt and Company, 1959.

Hulme, T. E. "Mr. Epstein and the Critics," *The New Age,* XIV (December 25, 1913), 251–53.

Hutchins, Patricia. *Ezra Pound's Kensington.* Chicago: Henry Regnery Company, 1965.

Jackson, Thomas H. *The Early Poetry of Ezra Pound.* Cambridge, Mass.: Harvard University Press, 1969.

Kennedy, Charles W. *The Earliest English Poetry.* New York: Oxford University Press, 1943.

Kennedy, Charles W., tr. *An Anthology of Old English Poetry.* New York: Oxford University Press, 1960.

Kirkwood, G. M. *A Short Guide to Classical Mythology.* New York: Rinehart and Company, 1959.

Leary, Lewis, ed. *Motive and Method in the Cantos of Ezra Pound.* New York: Columbia University Press, 1954.

Lewis, Wyndham P. "The Rock Drill," in *Ezra Pound Perspectives*, ed. by Noel Stock. Chicago: Henry Regnery Company, 1965. Pp. 198–202.

Lipscomb, Andrew A., ed. *The Writings of Thomas Jefferson*. Washington, D.C.: The Thomas Jefferson Memorial Association, 1905.

Mathews, R. H. *A Chinese-English Dictionary*. Shanghai: China Inland Mission and Presbyterian Mission Press, 1931.

Meacham, Harry M. *The Caged Panther: Ezra Pound at Saint Elizabeth's*. New York: Twayne Publishers, Inc., 1967.

Moritz, Charles, ed. *Current Biography Yearbook*. New York: H. W. Wilson Company, 1934.

Mullins, Eustace. *This Difficult Individual, Ezra Pound*. New York: Fleet Publishing Company, 1961.

Norman, Charles. *The Case of Ezra Pound*. New York: The Bodley Press, 1948.

——*Ezra Pound*. New York: Macmillan, 1968.

Olson, Paul A. "Pound and the Poetry of Perception," *Thought*, XXXV (Autumn, 1960), 331–48.

Orage, A. R. *The Art of Reading*. New York: Farrar & Rinehart, 1930.

Pearce, Roy Harvey. *The Continuity of American Poetry*. Princeton, N.J.: Princeton University Press, 1961.

Propertius, Sextus. *Sex. Propertii Elegia*. tr. by Lucianus Mueller. Leipzig: Teubner, 1910.

Putnam, George Haven. *Books and Their Makers during the Middle Ages*. 2 vols. New York: G. P. Putnam's Sons, 1896.

Read, Forrest. *Pound/Joyce*. New York: New Directions, 1967.

Reck, Michael. *Ezra Pound: A Close-up*. New York: McGraw-Hill Book Company, 1967.

Richard of St. Victor. *Benjamin Minor*. Tr. by S. V. Yankowski. Ansbrach: Wiefield & Mehl, 1960.

Rock, Joseph F. "The ² Muan ¹ Bpö Ceremony—or the Sacrifice to Heaven as Practiced by the ¹ Na- ²khi," *Monumenta Serica*, XIII (1948), 1–160.

Schneidau, Herbert N. *Ezra Pound: The Image and the Real*. Baton Rouge: Louisiana State University Press, 1969.

Sievert, William. *The Poetry of Ezra Pound*. New York: Monarch Press, 1965.

Spencer, Benjamin T. "Pound: The American Strain," *PMLA*, LXXXI (December, 1966), 457–66.

Stock, Noel. *The Life of Ezra Pound*. New York: Pantheon Books, 1970.

——*Reading the Cantos*. New York: Pantheon Books, 1966.

Stock, Noel, ed. *Ezra Pound Perspectives: Essays in Honor of His Eight-ieth Birthday.* Chicago: Henry Regnery Company, 1965.

Stokes, Adrian. *Stones of Rimini.* London: Faber & Faber, 1934.

Sullivan, J. P. *Ezra Pound and Sextus Propertius: A Study in Creative Translation.* Austin: University of Texas Press, 1964.

Sutton, Walter, ed. *Ezra Pound: A Collection of Critical Essays.* Engle-wood Cliffs, N.J.: Prentice-Hall, Inc., 1965.

Symonds, John Addington. *The Age of the Despots.* New York: G. P. Putnam's Sons, 1960.

Von Rad, Gerhard. *Old Testament Theology.* Vol. I. Tr. by D. M. G. Stalker. New York: Harper and Row, 1962.

Wang, John C. "Ezra Pound as a Translator of Classical Chinese Po-etry," *Sewanee Review,* XXXIII (Summer, 1965), 345–57.

Williams, William Carlos. *Autobiography.* New York: Random House, 1951.

Wright, George T. *The Poet in the Poem: The Personae of Eliot, Yeats, and Pound.* Berkeley: University of California Press, 1960.

Writers at Work: The Paris Review Interviews. Ed. by George Plimpton: with an introduction by Van Wyck Brooks. Vol. II. New York: The Viking Press, 1963.

Index